Initiative to Stop the Violence

World Thought in Translation

A joint project of Yale University Press and the MacMillan Center for International and Area Studies at Yale University, World Thought in Translation makes important works of classical and contemporary political, philosophical, legal, and social thought from outside the Western tradition available to English-speaking scholars, students, and general readers. The translations are annotated and accompanied by critical introductions that orient readers to the background in which these texts were written, their initial reception, and their enduring influence within and beyond their own cultures. World Thought in Translation contributes to the study of religious and secular intellectual traditions across cultures and civilizations.

Initiative to Stop the Violence

Mubādarat Waqf al-'Unf

Sadat's Assassins and the Renunciation of Political Violence

al-Gamā'ah al-Islāmīyah

Translated by Sherman A. Jackson

Yale UNIVERSITY PRESS
New Haven and London

This publication was made possible in part by a grant from the Carnegie Corporation of New York. The statements made and views expressed are solely the responsibility of the author.

Yale University Press books may be purchased in quantity for educational, business, or promotional use. For information, please e-mail sales.press@yale.edu (U.S. office) or sales@yaleup.co.uk (U.K. office).

Designed by Lindsey Voskowsky. Set in Adobe Caslon Pro and Whitney type by Integrated Publishing Solutions. Printed in the United States of America.

Library of Congress Cataloging-in-Publication Data

Hāfiz, Usāmah Ibrāhīm.
[Mubadārat waqf al-'unf. English]
Initiative to stop the violence : Sadat's assassins and the renunciation of political violence / al-Gamā'ah al-Islāmīyah ; translated by Sherman Jackson.
pages cm. — (World thought in translation)
Includes bibliographical references and index.
ISBN 978-0-300-19677-1 (hardback)
1. Peace—Religious aspects—Islam. 2. Jihad. 3. Gama'a al-Islamiyah (Organization) I. Gama'a al-Islamiyah (Organization) II. Title.
BP190.5.P34H3413 2014
363.3250962'09046—dc23

2014014245

A catalogue record for this book is available from the British Library.

This paper meets the requirements of ANSI/NISO Z39.48-1992 (Permanence of Paper).

10 9 8 7 6 5 4 3 2 1

To the Michigan Community,
With deeply cherished memories and eternal thanks

He responded, “I did that while I
was among those who are misguided.”
(26:20)

Contents

Preface

The tumultuous events that have gripped Egypt since the January 2011 revolution have raised many questions. Among the most disquieting has been whether the country would be thrown back into the kind of Islamist violence it experienced during the 1980s and 1990s. Those decades were the "heyday" of the notorious *al-Gamā'ah al-Islāmīyah,* and from the time they declared their decision to renounce political violence in 1997 (the subject of this book) suspicions regarding their sincerity have ebbed and flowed. But if ever there were circumstances that might reinstate violence as their primary medium of exchange, the chaos, brutality, and direct targeting of Islamists following the July 2013 ousting of president Mohammed Morsi would certainly seem to qualify. Yet, through all of this, the *Gamā'ah* has maintained its commitment to nonviolence, and its public statements and gestures suggest an ideological resolve to stay the course.

For weeks following the bloody removal of pro-Morsi supporters from *Rābi'ah al-'Adawīyah* square in August of 2013, the *Gamā'ah*'s official website streamed the following: "Stopping bloodshed is *the* religious obligation of our time and *the* form of religious devotion of our era, being superior to any other supererogatory act of worship." Meanwhile, news reports around this period have them condemning attacks on military forces in Sinai (even as they enjoin the army to "stay out of politics"), and denouncing attacks on Christian churches.[1] This is in addition to various commentaries by prominent members of the *Gamāʿah* that underscore the fallacy of wanton violence as an approach to change. All of this is consistent with the message of the work under review, which repudiates political violence as a primary language of negotiation.

Yet, the future remains far from predictable. For, beyond the radically changed fortunes of Egypt's Islamists in general, it is difficult to ignore or assess the impact of the military government's mass arrests and torture of prisoners. As the *Gamāʿah* points out in this and other works, this was a major contributor to the radicalization, resentment, and thirst for revenge that seized thousands of young Islamists in the 1970s and 1980s.[2] And this played an obvious role in the cycle of violence that rocked the country in the 1980s and early 1990s. For now, however, the *Gamāʿah* appears to be firm in its commitment to nonviolence. Given the present circumstances in Egypt, we can only hope—and some of us will pray—that they continue along this path.

Acknowledgments

We live in a post-9/11 world. And as we try to adjust to new regimes of legal accountability, we often find ourselves wrestling with questions that never crossed our minds during the "age of innocence." This book took a longer time—a much longer time—to come to press than my experience suggested should have been the case. And it was only the dedication and support of a number of key people that ultimately saw it through. First and foremost is Yale University Press editor William Frucht. Bill (I came to know him as such over the more than two years through which we labored together on this project) has been a model of professionalism, courage, and commitment. Even when things were looking their worst, he was there with a steady hand and a cool word of encouragement. Words are all I have here to express my gratitude. So let me say, with as much meaning and sincerity that words alone can convey: "Thank you, Bill. I appreciate your every effort." I must also thank Andrew March, who first invited me a few years ago to consider doing something for the Series. Like Bill, Andrew has been there every step of the way, always willing to offer whatever he could to move the process forward. Words of thanks are also due to Jonathan (J. A. C.) Brown, who took an interest in the project and was willing to use his offices to facilitate the publication of this book.

Finally, I must acknowledge and thank my family, Hassan, Shihab, Saphia, Niyyah, and my wife, Heather, for all of their sacrifice, support, and understanding, and for simply putting up with me—the distracted dad and husband—throughout the writing of this book and all the setbacks and difficulties that accompanied its eventual publication.

Introduction

Sherman A. Jackson

For more than a decade now, the tragic terror attacks of September 11, 2001, have dominated Western thinking, discourses, and sentiments about Islam, especially those articulations of the religion that value or prioritize public recognition of *sharīʿah* as the basis of Muslim law, politics, and society. In this context, the negative associations spawned by the specter of *al-Qāʿidah,* Usāmah b. Lādin (until recently), the Ṭālibān, Ayman al-Ẓawāhirī, or even the Muslim Brotherhood have occupied so much of our collective psychological space that they have left little room for recognizing variety, discord, or evolution in the thought, activities, or aspirations of contemporary Islamist movements. Understandably, this has weakened our ability to discern any substantive differences between those who express their commitment to Islam in ways that threaten America's security and those whose Islamic commitments simply go against this or that purported American ideal. And yet, failure to appreciate this distinction not only blinds us to the presence of potential allies or constructive interlocutors,[1] it can generate and sustain disproportionate levels of fear and what Amitai Etzioni refers to as "Multiple Realism Deficiency Disorder (MRDD)."[2] In the end, all of this can congeal into the self-fulfilling prophesy that greater adherence to Islam can only imply greater danger for America and the West.

Among the most spectacular blind spots generated by this frame of mind is one that has blocked from view one of the most unanticipated and potentially far-reaching developments in the history of modern, radical, jihadist thought:[3] the explicitly *sharī'ah*-based reassessment of political violence and its consequent renunciation as a means of advancing the Islamist cause. This landmark, which was inaugurated by Egypt's notorious *al-Gamā'ah al-Islāmīyah,* one of the largest,[4] most deadly, and ideologically committed Islamist cum-jihadist movements in the Muslim world, is now (in 2014) more than a decade and a half old. Yet, to date, it has received alarmingly scant attention among academics and or public intellectuals writing in English—especially when compared to the spectacular notice given to anything associated with Usāmah b. Lādin or *al-Qā'idah,* despite the *Gamā'ah*'s presumably much larger numbers and its incontrovertibly longer tenure as an organization.[5]

This book is an attempt to contribute to filling this lacuna by introducing the English-speaking world to the first and foundational installment in a series of corrective manifestos issued by *al-Gamā'ah al-Islāmīyah* a few years after it announced its decision to abandon political violence in 1997. This tract, entitled, *Mubādarat waqf al-ʿunf: Ruʾyah wāqiʿīyah wa naẓrah sharʿīyah,* a full translation of which I present here under the title *Initiative to Stop the Violence: A Reality-Based Assessment and a* Shariʿah-*Based Approach,* is the most seminal contribution to the group's new ideological orientation. In this capacity, it provides useful insight into the very meaning of the decision to abandon political violence and reflects a presumably permanent shift in doctrine, as opposed to a merely tactical maneuver of limited duration. Of course, this dizzying reorientation would produce its share of doubters, critics, and opponents, both within and without the *Gamāʿah,* even leading, in the former case, to a number of outright defections. Still, from the time of its inauguration in 1997, the *Gamāʿah* has doggedly pressed on with its reform effort, producing in the process some two dozen books,[6] all aimed at clarifying, deepening, defending, or expanding various aspects of its new understanding. Precisely what impact this will have on the future of jihadist thought overall is a question to which I shall return briefly in the penultimate section of this introduction. For now, I should like to provide a more concrete backdrop against which to appreciate the thrust, evolution, and significance of the *Gamāʿah*'s Initiative, as well as the *sharīʿah*-based justifications it relied upon to authenticate and sustain this reform approach.

Historical Evolution

On October 6, 1981, the entire world was shocked by the brash and audacious spectacle of Egyptian President Anwar Sadat's assassination. As he sat proudly before a celebratory procession of Egyptian military might, armed zealots fired upon the president in broad daylight from an ominously stopped military transport vehicle, from which they proceeded to storm the reviewing stand and, tossing incendiary devices, extended their automatic weapons over the partition in an effort to spray death upon a veritable who's who of Egyptian government. This was part of a plan to take over the country and establish an "Islamic state," the legal, social, economic, and political order of which would be explicitly defined and regulated by *sharīʿah*.[7] Coming as it did amid such unprecedented eruptions as the 1979 Islamic revolution in Iran, the 1979 seizure of the Grand Mosque in Mecca, and the 1983 bombing of the marine barracks in Beirut, this brazen effort joined that chorus of outbreaks that consummated the full arrival of modern Islamic militant activism, the ultimate, radical expression of which would precipitate, just two decades later, the most devastating, infamous, and epoch-making act of nonstate violence of our time.

Sadat's assassination had been orchestrated by an amalgamation of militant Islamic groups brought together the previous year under the forceful and charismatic leadership of a twenty-seven-year-old electrical engineer named Muḥammad ʿAbd al-Salām Faraj. Though not known to have received any formal *sharīʿah* training, Faraj had recently completed a bold and incendiary tract entitled *The Neglected Duty* (*al-Farīḍah al-ghāʾibah*),[8] in which he invoked the religious law and tradition to condemn the Egyptian state as an apostate regime, based on its failure-cum-unwillingness to rule according to *sharīʿah*. On this dereliction, Faraj insisted that Muslims had a religious duty—which they consistently ignored—to overthrow this anti-Islamic order by way of violent jihad.

To this end, Faraj established a clandestine group in Cairo that became known as Egyptian Jihad Incorporated (*Tanẓīm al-Jihād al-Miṣrī*), or more simply, Jihad Incorporated (*Tanẓīm al-Jihād*). Perhaps intentionally, this particular naming confused the relationship between this organization and another group that carried the same name but was established back in 1966.[9] While Faraj had for a time been associated with the earlier group, the latter had splintered, and in 1979 government pressure born of compromises to its secrecy had forced it to disband. According to ʿAbd al-Munʿim Munīb, an Islamist journalist who spent prison time with radical jihadists in the early 1980s and then consecutively from 1993 to 2007,[10] the original Jihad Inc. was reconstituted in 1980, not by Faraj but by Ayman al-Ẓawāhirī, ʿIṣām al-Qamarī, and Sayyid Imām (aka Dr. Faḍl).[11] Based on testimonies of arrested members following Sadat's assassination,[12] Faraj appears to have emerged as leader of a *separate* group that eventually evolved into a coalition that included members of both the original *and* the newly constituted Jihad Inc., in addition to a burgeoning coterie of new recruits. Chief among the more formally constituted groups joining this effort was a group headed by Kamāl al-Saʿīd Ḥabīb, as well as, above all, *al-Gamāʿah al-Islāmīyah*.[13] Under Faraj's leadership, all of these groups and individuals identified collectively, at least for a time, as Jihad Inc.[14]

At the time, *al-Gamāʿah al-Islāmīyah* was essentially a student organization that began in Upper Egypt and spread to other universities in the early to mid-1970s.[15] By the late 1970s, its ranks had grown to include middle-class engineers, lawyers, doctors, and teachers, alongside students, semi-educated youth, and uneducated peasants.[16] Its reputation as an ardent promoter of "Islamic" ideals and public morals, especially on university campuses and even more especially against communists and Nasserists, would prompt the Muslim Brotherhood (*al-Ikhwān al-Muslimūn*) to try to co-opt it. Though influenced and even inspired by the Brotherhood, the *Gamāʿah* would ultimately demur,[17] partly out of a youthful disdain for the senior organization's diminished appetite for physical confrontation.[18] Under the charismatic leadership of Karam Zuhdī, also known for his forceful personality and strident radicalism,[19] the *Gamāʿah* embraced Faraj's vision of violent jihad soon after meeting the Cairene bricoleur in 1980.[20] Within the coalition, however, the *Gamāʿah* continued to see itself, and to be seen, as the "Upper Egypt faction." But even on this distinction, its leaders would play a palpably critical role as part of the innermost circle of Faraj's Jihad Inc.

In 1981, it was actually the Cairo faction under the leadership of Faraj that carried out the assassination of Sadat (though Faraj himself was only an "instigator," not an actual participant).[21] Zuhdī and the Upper Egypt contingent were involved in what was to be a parallel mission in which they were to take over the city of Asyūṭ and from there move northward, gobbling up cities along the way for a grand crescendo in Cairo with Faraj and company.[22] Complications delayed things, however, and the Upper Egypt wing did not actually move on its plan until October 8 (the first day, incidentally, of *Eid al-Aḍḥā*, the four-day celebration winding down the Ḥajj or Pilgrimage to Mecca).[23] While the Cairo faction succeeded in its mission (as a result of which Faraj, Khālid al-Islāmbūlī and three others were executed),[24] the Upper Egypt faction's almost comical, if deadly,[25] execution resulted in Zuhdī and other leaders and members of the *Gamāʿah* being arrested and given stiff prison sentences.[26]

In prison, internal differences led to the eventual dissolution of the Cairo–Upper Egypt coalition. Jihad Inc, that is, the Cairo faction, virtually collapsed,[27] and *al-Gamā'ah al-Islāmīyah* resumed its status as an autonomous organization.[28] This was also the beginning, however, of a new phase in the *Gamā'ah*'s organizational infrastructure, a more explicit and formal doctrinal commitment, and an inexorably more confrontational relationship with the Egyptian state and society. Organizationally, the group developed a sophisticated plan to increase its numbers, coherence, and effectiveness. Already a strict hierarchy led by Zuhdī and the Consultative Council (*Majlis al-Shūrā*),[29] imprisoned members were assigned specific tasks based on the length of their sentences. Those who were to be released in three years were to devote themselves to missionary work, *da'wah,* to increase *Gamā'ah* numbers. Those to be released in five years were to expand the movement's organizational structure, including the installation of *amīr*s (field commanders), the establishment of subsidiary consultative councils and the physical location of alternative bases of operation. Those who were to be released in seven years were responsible for directing these new numbers and this expanded organizational capacity to the implementation of the movement's military operations.[30]

Alongside this logistical arrangement, the early prison period witnessed the production of pamphlets or "catechisms" designed to explain *Gamā'ah* doctrine, teach this to new recruits, and carry the movement's ideology to posterity. In the early period, the top leadership suspected that they would soon be executed or tortured to death. Thus, some of these books were written in haste. Even those that were not, however, reflected the rigidity and bitterness of the harsh prison experience, sparing nothing, as some of their titles clearly indicate, in laying out the movement's radical, jihadist outlook. Among the main titles were *Charter of Islamic Action* (*Mīthāq al-'amal al-islāmī;* 1984); *The Party That Desists from*

Applying a Rule of the Sharīʿah *of Islam* (*al-Ṭāʾifah al-mumtaniʿah ʿan sharīʿah min sharāʾiʿ al-islām;* 1988); *Does Another God Preside alongside God? A Declaration of War against Parliament* (*ʾA ilāhun maʿa Allāh: Iʿlān al-ḥarb ʿalā majlis al-shaʿb;* 1990); *The Inevitability of Confrontation* (*Ḥatmīyat al-muwājahah;* 1990); *A Message to All Who Operate in Accordance with Islam* (*Risālah ilā kulli man yaʿmal bi al-islam;* 1991).[31] As Salwā al-ʿAwwā points out in her informative study of the *Gamāʿah,* these works, in full or in part, ultimately reached the outside, where they would serve as the veritable constitution of field commanders and rank-and-file members.[32]

These books, however, like the infrastructural developments within the *Gamāʿah,* ultimately reflected the movement's attempt to adjust to an inexorably deteriorating and ominously confrontational relationship with the Egyptian state and society. Traditionally, the *Gamāʿah* had maintained a firm commitment to *daʿwah,* or religious preaching, the aim of which was to call Egyptians back to Islam. In fact, the whole point of establishing an Islamic state was to promote this very cause. In the context, however, of an Egypt still wrestling with its Islamic identity after more than a century of Western influence and domination, overzealousness on the part of *Gamāʿah* members, reciprocated by swift retaliation and occasionally overreaction by non-Muslim or government forces, routinely resulted in a spiral of violence. By the late 1980s, the sheer viciousness and volume of these confrontations had significantly blurred the *Gamāʿah*'s vision, both ideological and tactical. Especially among new recruits and field commanders, vendetta-style violence was rapidly establishing itself as a first-order principle, the *daʿwah* and pursuit of an Islamic state quietly receding to the margin.

Sadat's assassination and the Asyūṭ mission had awakened Egyptian authorities to the presence of something fundamentally new in their midst. This naturally informed their response to *Gamā'ah* activity, especially in the south, where Coptic-Muslim clashes in places like Asyūṭ, Dayrūṭ, and surrounding areas led to violent confrontations between the *Gamā'ah* and police and state security forces. This soon spread to other cities, such as al-Minyā, Banī Swayf, Fayūm, and even Cairo.[33] Over the next decade, the death toll would climb into the hundreds if not thousands,[34] including *Gamā'ah* members, police and security forces, government officials, Western tourists, Coptic Christians, secular intellectuals, and innocent bystanders.[35] These figures would be far surpassed, however, by the number of *Gamā'ah* members arrested and sent to prison.[36]

The bloody confrontations between the *Gamā'ah* and the Egyptian state took a heavy toll on both sides. In 1989, the *Gamā'ah* sought to relieve some of this pressure by presenting the government with its so-called Six Demands, satisfaction of which would be reciprocated by a cessation of all violent campaigns. These included: (1) the release of *Gamā'ah* members who had not been convicted of crimes;[37] (2) ending the practice of taking women as hostages and abusing them in detention in an effort to get suspects to surrender; (3) an end to torture; (4) improving general prison conditions and access to medical treatment; (5) ending the practice of harassing *Gamā'ah* preachers and teachers on the outside; (6) lifting general restrictions on *Gamā'ah* mosques.[38] The government rejected these demands (as it did with later mediation attempts, e.g., in 1993), based on its rejection of the idea that there was any parity between the *Gamā'ah* and the sovereign state of Egypt, as acceptance of any such agreement might imply.[39]

This was followed by a veritable *Gamā'ah* blitzkrieg, which only intensified after the summary execution of their avowedly peaceful preacher, 'Alā' Muḥyī al-Dīn, in August of 1990.[40] In addition to police and security forces, the *Gamā'ah* now targeted high government officials.[41] In 1989, they made attempts on the lives of the ministers of the interior, Zakī Badr and 'Abd al-Ḥalīm Mūsā. In 1992, they assassinated speaker of the parliament, Rif'at Maḥjūb. In 1993, they tried to kill the minister of the interior, Ḥasan Alfī; the minister of information, Ṣafwat al-Sharīf; and the prime minister, 'Aṭif Ṣidqī. In 1995, they went international with an attempt on President Ḥusnī Mubārak himself, during an official visit to Addis Ababa. In the heat of this "war of attrition," *Gamā'ah* motivations increasingly reclined, however, on a desire to exact revenge, force changes in specific policies (particularly regarding the incarcerated), and send a message to their enemies. Islam, *sharī'ah,* and the establishment of the Islamic state may have contributed to post facto rationalizations. But these were clearly not the actual motivating factors in many if not most instances. Speaking in this regard and to the dislocations that characterized the period as a whole, twice imprisoned first-tier *Gamā'ah* leader Usāmah Ḥāfiẓ tries to explain: "The idea of changing the system of government, this was our original idea. It was there, but these events were not what we had . . . I mean, there is a big difference between the two. I mean, it is a way of thinking—the idea of changing the system of government by force. This was there. But that these events occurred for the purpose of changing the system of government, no, this was something different."[42]

Looking back, there was a growing sense that things had degenerated to the point that it was the exception rather than the rule that *Gamā'ah* violence was animated or executed on the basis of *sharī'ah*—or even *Gamā'ah*-principles themselves. Speaking, for example, of the hostilities that engulfed the southern town of Dayrūṭ in 1992, the imprisoned leadership would depict the whole saga as a pathetic concatenation of petty confrontations and vendettas that simply spiraled out control: "These events started with the Ṣanbū affair involving some Christians, which was a matter of vengeance pure and simple. Then a succession of actions, reactions, killings, and counterkillings followed, to the point that things ended up as they did, and it became extremely difficult to stop them."[43]

Not only had the original ideals (and idealism) of the *Gamā'ah* been compromised by this torrent of violence, the very scale, persistence, and chaotic ferocity of these events reflected a palpable weakness in the imprisoned leadership's ability to control or at times even influence second-tier lieutenants and rank-and-file members on the outside. Again, Usāmah Ḥāfiẓ: "A good number of these events transpired without there being any real agreement on them. . . . A large part of what happened did not express our true ideology. It was simply the events themselves that imposed these actions."[44]

Of course, this did not entirely reflect the vantage point of second-tier field commanders and rank-and-file actors on the ground, or even that of *all* of the imprisoned leadership. While vengeance, the passion to defend honor, and the desire to change policies and send a message to enemies clearly informed the *Gamā'ah*'s actions, equally important was what they perceived to be the un-Islamic—indeed, the patently anti-Islamic—conduct of police, security forces, prison authorities, and other state officials. On some level, these breaches almost had to reinforce their commitment to toppling the existing order and establishing their version of an Islamic one in its place. By the late 1980s, Egyptian prisons teemed with *Gamā'ah* members, and the horrors of incarceration, the draconian measures used by police in pursuit of arrests, the routine denial of medical treatment and decent living conditions, the practice of indefinitely detaining suspects and arbitrarily extending the sentences of convicts who had already served their term, the regular policy of trying *Gamāʿah* members in military as opposed to civilian courts, the humiliation of seeing homes violated and wives and female relatives used as bait and then abused in detention, the heavy restrictions placed on *Gamāʿah* mosques and preachers, not to mention the summary execution of some of the latter—all of this intensified the rank-and-file's moral outrage alongside a sense that Islam itself was under mortal attack. Indeed, under the stress of these trying conditions and the relentless confrontations that paralleled them, it would be difficult, if not impossible, for *Gamāʿah* members to distinguish *their* honor and interests from the honor and interests of Islam, indeed, their very survival from the survival of Islam. As both sides—the government and the *Gamāʿah*—believed unquestionably in the righteousness of its cause, during the early to mid-1990s there was no end in sight to the deadly, unremitting, and absolutely haunting violence that raged between them.[45]

The Initiative to Stop the Violence and the *Gamāʿah*'s Reassessment

It was in this context that, on July 5th, 1997, rank-and-file *Gamāʿah* member Muḥammad al-Amīn ʿAbd al-ʿAlīm, stunned the nation. At his trial before a military tribunal on charges of blowing up banks, he stood up in open court and read a statement to which six first-tier, imprisoned *Gamāʿah* leaders had attached their signatures:[46] "The Historical Leadership of *al-Gamā'ah al-Islāmīyah* calls upon their brethren from among the leadership and the rank-and-file to terminate, without stipulation and with no prerequisites, all armed campaigns and all communiqués that call for such, both inside and outside of Egypt, in the interest of Islam and the Muslims."[47]

This was the formal inauguration of the so-called Initiative to Stop the Violence.[48] It also reflected, however, the results of an ongoing effort within the imprisoned *Gamā'ah* leadership to steer the movement away from the shallow pragmatism and reactionary tendencies of its past toward a reassessment of its activities in light of *sharī'ah*. These efforts culminated just a few years later in the issuance of four manifestos under the series title *Correcting Misunderstandings* (*Silsilat taṣḥīḥ al-mafāhīm*), all of which first appeared in 2002. As their titles suggest, these writings were explicitly designed to refute the old commitment to violence as the primary medium of exchange, vindicate the Initiative to Stop the Violence, set the *Gamā'ah* on a new (or renewed) *sharī'ah*-based ideological foundation, and repair the group's relationship with the Egyptian state and society. The series included the following titles:

1. *Initiative to Stop the Violence: A Reality-Based Assessment and a* Sharī'ah-*Based Approach* (*Mubādarat waqf al-'unf: Ru'yah wāqi'īyah wa naẓrah shar'īyah*)
2. *Shedding Light on the Mistakes That Have Befallen* (*the Understanding of*) *Jihad* (*Taslīṭ al-aḍwā' 'alā mā waqa'a fī al-jihād min al-akhṭā'*)
3. *Advice and Clarification to Correct Misunderstandings Among Those Who Police Public Morals* (*al-Nuṣḥ wa al-tabyīn fī taṣḥīḥ mafāhim al-muḥtasibīn*)

4. *The Impermissibility of Religious Extremism and of Declaring Fellow Muslims to Be Infidels* (*Ḥurmat al-ghulūw fī al-dīn wa takfīr al-muslimīn*)

These tracts were all issued as joint publications. Two or three members of the Consultative Council—not always the same members—would write a tract, and the remaining five or six would review and endorse it.[49] The tracts were then sent to al-Azhar seminary, with no names attached, for official review and authentication. Al-Azhar's Council for Islamic Research (*Majma' al-Buḥūth al-Islāmīyah*) issued written appraisals of each tract, registering minor criticisms and suggestions but ultimately concluding that there was nothing in these booklets that contradicted the teachings of Islam.[50] The eight leaders whose names appear on all these booklets include:

1. Karam Muḥammad Zuhdī (1953) (2003)
2. 'Alī Muḥammad 'Alī al-Sharīf (1956) (2004)
3. Ḥamdī 'Abd al-Raḥmān 'Abd al-Aẓīm (1953) (2001)
4. 'Āṣim 'Abd al-Mājid Muḥammad (1958) (2011?)
5. Nājiḥ Ibrāhīm 'Abd Allāh (1953) (2005)
6. Usāmah Ibrāhīm Ḥāfiẓ (1953) (2004)
7. Fu'ād Muḥammad al-Dawālībī (1953) (2005)
8. Muḥammad 'Iṣām al-Dīn Darbālah (1957) (2006)[51]

While Zuhdī was clearly *the* leader, all of these men had been part of the top decision-making body, the *Majlis al-Shūrā* or Consultative Council, going back to the days of 'Abd al-Salām Faraj.[52] By this time, however, the organization had swollen to include literally thousands of second-tier leaders and rank-and-file members, some of whom were unborn or still minor children at the time of the Asyūṭ mission and Sadat's assassination. As the actual founders of the *Gamā'ah* who had established and burnished its reputation, the imprisoned forerunners enjoyed an undeniable pride of place. They were now asserting this advantage and pointing up a certain deference due them by explicitly identifying themselves as the "Historical Leadership" (*al-Qādah al-Tarīkhīyūn*) of the *Gamā'ah*. This was part of an attempt to parlay their prestige into the twin goals of redirecting *Gamā'ah* ideology and seeing the Initiative to Stop the Violence to full acceptance and implementation.

Challenges and Responses

From the beginning, however, the Historical Leadership faced challenges, both within and without the *Gamā'ah*. Within the *Gamā'ah*, even members of the Consultative Council who eventually signed the manifestos initially hesitated to go along with the Initiative.[53] Outside the organization there was the question of the *Gamā'ah*'s credibility among rival Islamists, on the one side, and the disquieting doubts and aspersions cast by the general public and government officials, on the other. The *Gamā'ah* leadership would work feverishly to overcome these deficits, and the series of manifestos would play a major role in this regard. Still, the road to universal (or perhaps more accurately general) acceptance on an ideological as opposed to a merely tactical level was extremely bumpy and extended for several years after the initial declaration.

The first blow to the *Gamā'ah*'s efforts came just a few months after the announcement of the decision to renounce political violence. On November 17, 1997, a *Gamā'ah* faction massacred some fifty-eight Western tourists and a handful of Egyptians at the temple of Hepshatsut in Luxor. The Historical Leadership would later describe this as a "hard stab in our backs,"[54] and speak of how deeply demoralized they were by it. Expectedly, this ruthless attack raised serious doubts among the general public and even prompted the minister of the interior to go on record denouncing the Initiative as a cheap ploy in pursuit of pardons and sentence reductions.[55] Within the *Gamā'ah,* meanwhile, prominent members such as Rifā'ī Ṭāhā, a long-standing, second-tier field commander, praised the massacre. At the time, Ṭāhā was in Afghanistan, where he had gone upon his release from prison (as a 'fiver') around 1986 to join the jihad against the Soviets and expand the *Gamā'ah*'s organizational base. A big believer in the use of violence as a bargaining chip, his opposition to the Initiative was primarily, though not exclusively, tactical. Specifically, he feared that such a "show of weakness" would send the wrong message to the Egyptian government, the rank-and-file, *and* potential recruits. In this light, he counted the Luxor mission a success and saw it as both exerting needed pressure on the government and burnishing the *Gamā'ah*'s jihadist bona fides.[56] As he headed the Consultative Council abroad, this was clearly a problem for the Historical Leadership, as Ṭāhā was a master-organizer who had "massive weight among many brothers."[57] Their differences with Ṭāhā eventually prompted the latter to join Usāmah b. Lādin's International Front for Jihad against Jews and Crusaders in 1998, and sign the infamous *fatwā* in which Bin Lādin called for the indiscriminate killing of Americans.[58]

Despite this obvious setback, the Historical Leadership pressed on. And it may have been, ironically, the Luxor massacre that gradually enabled them to solidify a modicum of agreement among the upper echelons, second-tier leadership, and influential "ground troops." Simply stated, the brutality and gruesomeness of the affair (killing women and children, mutilating their bodies) simply offended the sensibilities of many and confirmed their growing suspicion that something was amiss. As a result, the following year witnessed a steady stream of endorsements that overshadowed the opposition of the likes of Rifāʿī Ṭāhā,[59] Usāmah Rushdī, and Muḥammad Shawqī al-Islambūlī (brother of Khālid), all old-guard stalwarts who went back to the days of ʿAbd al-Salām Faraj and the coalition.[60] On this development, the Historical Leadership would announce that on March 19, 1999, even the leadership abroad had issued a statement that resulted in what they counted as "full agreement" (*al-taʾyīd al-kāmil*) on the Initiative.[61]

On a tactical level, this was likely at least close to true. As Omar Ashour points out in his informative article, the Luxor massacre "was the last violent act perpetrated by IG [*Gamāʿah*] affiliates."[62] This, however, was only the tactical front. By early 1999, the ideological battle remained far from over. Even if *Gamāʿah* members and second-tier field commanders had come to agree that their erstwhile commission of political violence was now tactically unwise, this was not the same as agreeing that it was religiously proscribed (*ḥarām*). Nor would this recognition alone be enough to displace the truculent *fiqh al-ʿunf*, or "jurisprudence of violence," that the Historical Leadership had produced early on and used to indoctrinate rank-and-file members for so many years. In short, turning the ideological ship around would require much bigger oars and some much more powerful oaring. This may explain why the Historical Leadership placed so much stock in the timely overtures by the (in)famous blind cleric, Shaykh ʿUmar ʿAbd al-Raḥmān.[63]

In early 1999, Shaykh 'Umar, who had been implicated in the 1993 World Trade Center bombing, sent word from his jail cell in New York expressing his approval of the Initiative.[64] While certain members of the now dislocated *Jihad Inc.* had issues with Shaykh 'Umar, he was an Upper Egyptian, his and the wife of Karam Zuhdī were full sisters, and, as an Azharī, he had a long-standing relationship with the *Gamā'ah* as their religious guide.[65] Beyond this, he was a respected figure in jihadist circles overall who had even traveled to Afghanistan and plugged into the burgeoning networks there. Clearly, his endorsement would go a long way in offsetting Islamist criticisms within and without the *Gamā'ah.* In fact, it might even mitigate some of the misgivings of secularists and government officials. For, especially following his brash performance at his 1982 trial, Shaykh 'Umar had acquired unimpeachable bona fides as an absolutely uncompromising Islamist.[66] If he was willing to put his Islamist bona fides on the line, the Initiative had to be more than sheer window dressing, and it had to have a clear and reliable basis in the religious law.

While it is reasonable, however, to assume that Shaykh 'Umar's opinion was important, it was clearly not dispositive. For one, the shaykh went back and forth on the matter, originally supporting the Initiative, then withdrawing support, upon learning of a number of *Gamā'ah* members being killed by security forces.[67] This was followed by two expressions of disapproval, in May and June 2000, only to be followed by a more neutral statement in which he advised the Consultative Council to do as it saw fit.[68] Thus, as late as the summer of 2000, Shaykh 'Umar was still mulling over the issue, and it is not entirely clear whether whatever support he ultimately offered was merely tactical or actually grounded in ideological commitment. Meanwhile, the Initiative and its theoretical underpinnings were still being fiercely debated within the *Gamā'ah* at large. Indeed, as late as June of 2000, according to the indictment of American attorney Lynne Stewart, who was accused and convicted of illegally passing messages back and forth from Shaykh 'Umar to the *Gamā'ah* (including his statements on the Initiative), Shaykh 'Umar's son, Muḥammad, is reported to have sought to convey a message to his father in which he informed the latter of the "fierceness of the debate."[69]

As late as the middle of 2000, then, the *Gamā'ah* had not realized anything near unanimous consensus on the ideological front. Ironically, however, it may have been the terror attacks of September 11, 2001, that took them the rest of the distance. In October 2001,[70] in the immediate aftermath and almost certainly as a response to the 9/11 attacks, the Egyptian government permitted and gave material support to a peripatetic tour by the Historical Leadership in which they traveled to various prisons around the country to clarify and debate the Initiative and its *sharī'ah*-based vindications with incarcerated second-tier and rank-and-file members. This campaign, which lasted some ten months, is described in a later book, *Memory Lane* (*Nahr al-dhikrāyāt*), written by the *Gamā'ah* leadership and published in 2003. This book includes moving descriptions of tearful reunions of *Gamā'ah* members who had been separated by prison walls for some twenty years, together with sad portraits of younger men, some barely in their twenties, decked out in red jump suits that marked them "dead men walking." Much of the information in this book is corroborated (and supplemented) by Makram Muḥammad Aḥmad, editor-in-chief of the chic and patently secular magazine *The Captured Image* (*al-Muṣawwar*). Aḥmad attended some of these sessions, interviewed imprisoned *Gamā'ah* leaders, and described all of this in his book *Conspiracy or Reassessment* (*Mu'āmarah aw murāja'ah*).[71] Coming as they did on the heels of all that had transpired and reclining against the backdrop of the *Gamā'ah*'s long and painful history, itself now amplified by a tragic demonstration of the wages of the very logic that underwrote that approach, it was in all likelihood *these* efforts that carried the Initiative to full doctrinal success and spelled the real end of the *Gamā'ah*'s ideological commitment to political violence.

Motivations

In her important study on the *Gamā'ah,* Salwā al-'Awwā cites three theories that have been put forth as possible explanations for why the imprisoned leadership embarked upon the Initiative: (1) they struck a deal with the Egyptian government in which both sides saw themselves as beneficiaries; (2) they simply caved in to government pressure to alter their ideology and practical agenda; (3) they underwent a genuine ideological shift in light of an internally driven, *sharī'ah*-based reassessment of their practical program and doctrinal profile. In reality, there can be little doubt that on some level *all* of these considerations informed the *Gamā'ah*'s decision, as well as the outcome of their effort. The real question is which of these influences was primary or determinative and which secondary or perhaps coincidental.

That the government appreciated the utility of the *Gamā'ah*'s reform effort and sought to turn this to its advantage is clear from its agreement to permit and lend material support to the peripatetic tour. Given the treatment traditionally meted out to imprisoned

Islamists, this was obviously the sweeter side of a carrot-and-stick policy, the other side including its share of tangible "disincentives," from torture to denying food, medical care, family visitations, and so on. Yet, it would be a stretch to jump from this to the conclusion that the *Gamā'ah*'s effort was little more than a "deal" or the result of the imprisoned leadership's "caving in."[72] For even if the *Gamā'ah* was *influenced* by government incentives and disincentives, this would not be the same as their being *motivated* by these, such that they would have attempted no reform at all in the absence of such considerations. The Historical Leaders have consistently denied that they were motivated by offers or overtures by the government, even as they acknowledge the role of the peripatetic tour and even the contributions of certain government officials, for example, Aḥmad Ra'fat, undersecretary of the state security apparatus, who eventually came to support the Initiative.[73] This claim is explicitly supported and, given his position and vantage point, one might say corroborated, by the aforementioned 'Abd al-Mun'im Munīb. As mentioned, Munīb spent almost a decade and a half in prison with members of the Historical Leadership. And while he goes to great lengths to avoid the appearance of bias in what he reports, he cannot fully suppress a certain irritation he nurses toward the *Gamā'ah*.[74] Yet, Munīb makes it clear that he was there at *Līmān Ṭurah* prison when the Initiative was first launched, and against the suggestion that the *Gamā'ah* hatched this effort in pursuit of pardons or sentence reductions or under duress or manipulation by prison or security officials, he states plainly:

> I know for a fact that it was Karam Zuhdī alone in the flesh who went on his own two feet to the officer from the state security apparatus who was posted at the prison and presented

to the latter the idea of a dialogue with the security apparatus. After that, he (Zuhdī) went on to develop the Initiative. As for the security apparatus then proceeding to promote the Initiative and nudge it in this direction or that, this is also true. But this does not negate the fact that the *Gamā'ah* leadership who agreed with the Initiative, both inside and outside the prison, proceeded on the basis of their own free choice.[75]

Elsewhere in his account, Munīb points up another detail that bears directly on the question of whether the *Gamā'ah* succumbed to government coercion or manipulation. While the Historical Leadership was clearly able to garner *enough* support to keep the Initiative alive, there remained *Gamā'ah* leaders and members, even inside prison, who disagreed.[76] Yet, despite their disagreement, any number of these men was subsequently released.[77] If coercion or manipulation were the source of the Historical Leadership's decision, why did these tactics summarily fail in the case of those imprisoned leaders and members who demurred? Conversely, while some of the leadership on the outside opposed the Initiative (e.g., Rifā'ī Ṭāhā, Usāmah Rushdī, Muḥammad Shawqī al-Islāmbūlī), others promptly agreed. Clearly, Munīb points out, the agreement of these leaders on the outside, some of whom were not even in Egypt at the time, could not have been coerced or manipulated by the government.[78] Again, while the Egyptian government clearly played *a* role in the overall saga of the Initiative, it was not the primary or decisive factor. Rather, I tend to agree with al-'Awwā when she suggests that by the time the *Gamā'ah* leadership came to announce the Initiative to Stop the Violence, they were seeking primarily neither to avoid repression nor garner favors from the government but rather to save *al-Gamā'ah al-Islāmīyah* from itself![79]

In his informative treatment of this question, however, Omar Ashour seems to think that government repression was a major, if not decisive, factor both in prompting the Initiative and in bringing it to success. Again, while I agree that repression undoubtedly play *a* role, I am not sure that Ashour is completely circumspect in considering exactly what role that might have been. Specifically, he appears to give short shrift to at least two important factors in light of which repression might actually promote the opposite effect, or prove to be tangentially relevant at best. The first of these is what one might call, for lack of a better term, the importance that incarcerated individuals routinely attach to their "jailhouse 'rep,'" that is, their reputation among the general prison population and even supporters and adversaries on the outside. The second consideration is the simple fact that the *Gamā'ah* was first and foremost a *religious* movement for whose members the appeal to religion would always be a factor influencing behavior. That circumstances, indoctrination, or personal experience might engender one understanding of an aspect of religion today and an opposite understanding tomorrow should not so unproblematically reduce us to the conclusion that religious belief always follows and never leads. Indeed, there seems to be little doubt that the *Gamā'ah*'s early catechisms, once accepted, played a major role in enabling members to legitimize their violent acts to themselves. I see no reason to assume that a changed doctrinal position, once accepted, would not be equally capable, on its own, of promoting the opposite effect. In fact, in the absence of such a change in religious *doctrine,* it is difficult to see how the Historical Leadership could have sustained their new ideological perspective as the doctrinal foundation of the "new" *Gamā'ah.*

Regarding the importance of "jailhouse rep," first-tier leader

Usāmah Ḥāfiẓ provides valuable insight into this reality. At the time the Initiative was first announced from *Līmān Ṭurah* prison, Ḥāfiẓ was actually in the south at *al-Wādī al-Jadīd* prison, where conditions were much worse. When "one of the brothers" asked him if he had heard about the Initiative he replied in the affirmative. The following exchange then ensues: "He then asked: 'What's your opinion about it?' I said to him: 'I don't have an opinion; I don't know anything about it (in terms of substance).' He followed: 'Okay, if you were invited to join it?' I said: 'Were I invited to join it while I'm here in *al-Wādī,* no way I would agree to it. Because I'm here in *al-Wādī,* it would be said about me that I buckled, because conditions here are so harsh. Now, were I to go *there* [i.e., *Līmān*], I'd have a different opinion.'"[80]

For Ḥāfiẓ, the repressive atmosphere at *al-Wādī al-Jadīd* actually had the effect of forestalling his endorsement of the Initiative. Indeed, he states elsewhere, reflecting what might be taken to be a common attitude among those in his position, "A person who is being tortured in prison—there is no way he can accept the Initiative, because he will be viewed by himself and by others as having betrayed his cause."[81] Again, this is not to say that torture, repression, and other disincentives would not cumulatively assert some effect on individuals' thinking. But that it would unilaterally and on a broad scale produce in ideologically committed, battle-hardened, incarcerated Egyptian Islamists an untempered, Pavlovian-type response calls, I think, for reconsideration. In fact, time and again, rank-and-file *Gamā'ah* members would insist that it was ultimately their unwavering certainty that Zuhdī and the imprisoned top brass would never give in to torture or any other form of government pressure that ultimately allowed them to endorse the Initiative in good conscience.[82]

As for the role of religiosity, al-ʿAwwā reminds us in her study that the primary motivation behind members' joining the *Gamāʿah* to begin with was religious conviction. Had it been purely political or economic or even social, there were plenty of other outlets to accommodate such commitments. In the early years, *Gamāʿah* leadership had actually taught members that their violent confrontations were not only consistent with religion but dictated by it. This, in fact, would become a major stumbling block in the months and years following the Initiative. Members asked openly about the early catechisms, about all the people (within and without the *Gamāʿah*) who had died, all the families that had been destroyed, all the members whose children had gone astray during their absence in prison, and how they could all now face God with this record of deeds.[83] Parallel to this, however, members register ever-creeping religious misgivings about their violent acts, misgivings they felt they could not express under the conditions and group dynamics of incarceration and the need to remain united in the face of a relentless, ubiquitous enemy. Nevertheless, these were there. And for many, the Initiative actually came as a relief, as it gave them permission to yield to the dictates of their religious conscience. As one member put it, "This was the reason that allowed many cadres of the *Gamāʿah* to except the Initiative, that is, that it articulated issues and questions that had already been percolating in their breasts."[84]

We get an even clearer glimpse into the quiet workings of religion on the psyche of *Gamāʿah* members through the testimony of Mamdūḥ ʿAlī Yūsuf, a fearless second-tier leader and field commander over military operations from 1987 to 1990. Mamdūḥ records an exchange between himself and a prison official at *Līmān Ṭurah* prison, which he visited from the much harsher *al-ʿAqrab* prison, where he had been held for a number of years. The prison official asks in a pointed and accusatory tone why the *Gamāʿah* had spilled so much blood and caused all this chaos and destruction. Mamdūḥ defiantly retorts that it was not the *Gamāʿah* but the repressive security apparatus that forced these events. The official then protests, now in an elongated, half-patronizing tone, "But Mamdūḥ, you are a man of religion," to which Mamdūḥ responds, "And?" The official continues, now half exasperated: "Even if *I* do something wrong, even if *I* violate the religion and do this or that, *you* are supposed to be a religious man; *you* are not supposed to violate the religion. How can you engage in acts that go against *sharīʿah*? Simply because *I* do?"[85]

Mamdūḥ relates that these words "shook me,"[86] reminding him that he was indeed bound by an independent criterion that he must not violate, even if others did. He recalls in this context the Prophet's statement, "Honor the trust of those who entrust you. And do not betray those who betray you."[87] Mamdūḥ reports that he confronted his superiors in the movement and asked them how he could now face God having engaged in all the violent acts he had. Rather than make excuses for themselves, however, or try to reinterpret their former writings to render them not "really" wrong, their willingness to admit their mistakes and throw themselves on God's mercy and forgiveness convinced him to do the same. From here he reports that when he engaged his comrades who were still diffident about the Initiative, he would say to them: "I am the one who did such and such. And I did such and such. And I never feared anything. And now I will not fear anything. God willing, God will sustain me, and I will not fear anything. And I will say that *what we did was wrong*, for reason 1, 2, 3 . . ."[88]

All of this brings us to the motivations most consistently cited by the leadership themselves: a reassessment of their ideological and practical commitments in light of what they came to understand of *sharīʿah.* As our translated text will show, during their years of imprisonment, the *Gamāʿah* leadership thoroughly familiarized themselves with the classical discourse on *sharīʿah* (not to mention an interesting array of modern Western works). Indeed, they limit themselves neither to a particular school of thought (*madhhab*) nor a particular era. Rather, the entire tradition presents itself as a cornucopia of sorts, from which they draw views in support of their new perspective. This raises the question, of course, of the extent to which *sharīʿah* actually *dictated* their new position or was simply *called upon to justify* conclusions already reached on other (e.g., practical) grounds. Ultimately, however, the question itself waxes moot. For once the *sharīʿah* justifications were pressed into service, they would effectively function as religious dictates. And once the commitment to wanton violence had been discredited on *sharīʿah* grounds, it would be religiously unacceptable for believing, fastidiously practicing Muslims, which *Gamāʿah* members so fervently prided themselves on being, to return to that approach.

The Main Argument

The mainstay of the Historical Leadership's argument was the quite classical Islamic legal principle of *maṣlaḥah,* or "the broader or underlying aims and objectives of the religious law,"[89] coupled with an emphasis on what has come to be known as *fiqh al-wāqiʿ,* i.e., "properly assessing and understanding reality."[90] The two tracts in their series of manifestos that deal most directly with political violence are *Initiative to Stop the Violence* (*Mubādarat waqf al-'unf*) and *Shedding Light on the Mistakes That Have Befallen (the Understanding of) Jihad* (*Taslīṭ al-aḍwā' 'alā mā waqa'a fī al-jihād min al-akhṭā'*). They begin with a discussion of benefits and liabilities and insist that Islamic law is inextricably bound to a balancing exercise that seeks to maximize benefits and minimize harms. Rather than assume, however, the existence of *pure* benefits and *pure* harms, the religious law seeks to accentuate *relative* benefit and minimize *relative* harm. Several proofs from the Qur'ān and Sunna are adduced in support of this. A typical example is the verse, "They ask you about wine drinking and games of chance. Say, in them is great vice, along with benefits for people; but their vice is greater than their benefit" (2:219). Wine drinking, as is well-known, is outlawed by the religious law, despite the Qur'ān's explicit admission of its marginal benefits.

This sets the stage for the major premise of the *Gamā'ah* leadership's argument, namely, that whenever the application of a rule threatens either to subvert the benefit it was intended to promote or accentuate a harm that it or the law in general was intended to avert, it becomes unlawful to apply that rule. Moreover, in assessing the impact of a rule's application, the avoidance of harm is to be given precedence over the procurement of benefit.[91] This is placed in tandem with what the *Gamā'ah* insists is the necessity of factoring real-life circumstances and likely consequences into any decision regarding the application of the religious law. The result of this filiation is the following conclusion: "It is clear error to assume positions, establish rulings, or issue *fatwā*s removed from a consideration of actual reality on the ground and a comprehensive assessment of its implications, considering this a fundamental pillar upon which *fatwās* must be based. Indeed, all rulings and all *fatwās* must recline upon two fundamental constituents: (1) reality on the ground and its implications; and (2) *sharī'ah*-proofs from the Qur'ān, Sunna, or other recognized sources of legislation."[92]

What *Gamā'ah* leaders are essentially arguing here is that their bloody confrontations with the Egyptian government did not realize any religiously recognized benefits. On the contrary, these hostilities brought nothing but harm, not simply to the *Gamā'ah* but to *all* Islamic movements, not to mention Egypt as a society and a regional Muslim power. In fact, the only ones to benefit from this chaos and destruction were those whose interests at the moment actually contradicted those of Islam: Israel, America, the West in general, expatriate Copts (*Aqbāṭ al-Mahjar*), and various groups of Egyptian secularists.[93] In other words, not only was the cumulative effect of their violence to mar the image of Islam and marginalize, if not undermine, Islamic discourse overall, it strengthened the hand of antireligious and anti-Islamic forces and heightened the latter's ability to scare and incite people against the religion via the specter of terrorism and antiterrorism rhetoric.[94] This comes to serve as the minor premise of the leadership's argument: wanton violence undermines the propagation of Islam. This in turn leads to their ultimate conclusion: *Jihad against the Egyptian state is not Islamically sanctioned.*

On its face, this might appear to be a rather facile, post facto argument grounded almost entirely in self-serving pragmatism. We know, in other words, that jihad against the Egyptian state is not sanctioned because we tried it and it didn't work. While there is clearly a pragmatic element to the *Gamā'ah*'s reasoning, it would be an exaggeration to cast it as unprincipled. For what the *Gamā'ah* is actually saying is that they *should* have known that Islam did not sanction their political violence, and they *would* have known this had they understood Islam itself to require them to anticipate the likely consequences of their acts. In other words, on a proper understanding of Islam, attempting to arrive at an accurate assessment of the real or likely implications of one's acts would have been recognized as a religious obligation. In fact, this *factual* assessment might prove to be just as probative—if not more probative—than one's understanding of scriptural *texts.* Failure to appreciate this was at the heart of the "misunderstanding" the *Gamāʿah* leadership now wants to correct. Indeed, in an interview in 2001, first-tier leader Ḥamdī ʿAbd al-Raḥmān, who was known in certain circles at the time as the *faqīh al-Gamāʿah* (jurist of the movement),[95] and who actually coauthored *Shedding Light on the Mistakes That Have Befallen (the Understanding of) Jihad,* summarized the matter as follows:

> The mistake we made in the past was that we used to privilege (individual) texts over the broader aims and objectives of the law, allowing the texts to run rough-shod over these aims and objectives. We used to engage in jihad without taking any account of the benefits or harms that would accrue to our action. Now, however, our understanding has changed: it is the broader aims and objectives that determine the application of the text. So if the text says, for example, wage jihad against the Jews, I must first determine the benefit to derive from this jihad, that is, will my [religion's] interests be realized by fighting or by not fighting. This is the sound approach [*wa hādhā huwa al-ṣaḥīḥ*].[96]

Of course, implied in all of this is the idea that jihad is not an end in itself but a means to some broader objective. This is precisely the *Gamā'ah*'s point. Throughout both these tracts, they repeatedly insist that jihad is but a means to an end. That end, in turn, is explicitly identified as "guiding humanity to God" (*hidāyat al-khalq ilā al-ḥaqq*).[97] This, they affirm, is the apex mission of the Muslim Community, which it inherited from the Prophet himself.[98] The job of those who undertake this mission is thus "to endear people to their Lord and Creator and direct them to the straight path of God, via the least burdensome means and the easiest route."[99] Violence, for its part, is only prescribed as a means of serving and protecting this basic mission. And inasmuch as it entails benefits (e.g., repelling aggression, making a show of force) and harms (taking life, destroying property), it can only be indulged to the extent that its benefits outweigh its harms. But, they note, "When jihad itself becomes a source of religious strife and an impediment to getting people to worship their Lord, blocking the path to the call to truth and scaring the youth away from the fruit of a clean call to the Faith, jihad does not realize its noble aim."[100]

In such case, the *Gamā'ah* concludes, jihad would be flatly forbidden, according to the religious law itself. For, "if it preponderates in one's thinking that jihad will not bring about the interest for which it was legislated, its legality is thereby nullified and it ceases to be a desideratum of the religious law. That is to say, the law and its machinery cease to address legally responsible Muslims with this obligation."[101]

To continue or insist on waging jihad under such circumstances would amount to jihad for the sake of jihad. But according to the *Gamā'ah*'s new understanding, "jihad that does not stand to realize its religiously sanctioned purpose constitutes extremism and stiff-necked rigidity [*ghulūw wa tashaddud*], which the religious law condemns."[102] This, again, was precisely the insight that their earlier understanding of jihad and its place in Islam had not included. In *Initiative to Stop the Violence,* this is extensively laid out in traditional *sharīʿah*-terms, as the leadership invokes a series of what classical Islamic law recognizes as "legal impediments" (*mawāniʿ*/ sg. *māniʿ*) to the application of otherwise perfectly valid rules.

Having said all of this, we should not mistake the *Gamāʿah* leadership to be relaxing its commitment to the sacred law, including the duty of jihad in its proper place, or to defending the *sharīʿah* against unwarranted compromise. They simply reject the notion that they must *apply* the law in some presumably ideal, Kantian mode,[103] with no regard for concrete sociopolitical reality and no responsibility for practical consequences. Of course, taken seriously, this sensitivity to societal consequences could be taken, at least by some, as a direct and inexorable path to secularization. For if the application of the religious law can be legitimately relaxed on the basis of likely outcome, modernity as a whole might be pointed to as a context in which the application of Islamic law will *always* entail prohibitively negative consequences. This is keenly captured in an exchange between Makram Muḥammad Aḥmad and Ḥamdī ʿAbd al-Raḥmān. While conceding that much of Egyptian law was consistent with *sharīʿah,* Ḥamdī notes that much of it was not, pointing specifically to such criminal sanctions as those governing adultery, fornication, and theft.[104] Aḥmad retorts that society has now changed and, given the *Gamāʿah*'s own insistence on the importance of sociopolitical reality to *sharīʿah*-deliberation, asks if such change should not warrant a change in these rules.

Ḥamdī's response is essentially that while social reality may affect the *application* of a particular rule, for example, by affecting whether or not the broader aims and objectives of the law are likely to be served, this does not necessarily affect the overall validity of a particular rule itself, any more than the authority of traffic lights is invalidated by the occasional need to ignore them in certain emergency situations. In addition, Ḥamdī intimates, there may be a difference between the broader aims and objectives of the law and society's appetitive wants and desires. Muslim society must be careful not to conflate its every want and desire with the broader aims and objectives of the religious law. Otherwise, it is likely to end up undermining the law, by rejecting or refusing to apply rules that frustrate societal "wants" or preferences even though they clearly serve the broader aims and objectives identified by the law itself. For Ḥamdī, Muslim society cannot arrogate to itself the right to say that a religious rule should not be applied simply because society does not like it. It may only set aside a rule where its application threatens to undermine the law's own self-determined objectives. Having said this much, however, Ḥamdī is willing to leave the question of whether and how much scripturally recognized harm will result from a rule's application to the authorities and basically not to second-guess them in this regard.[105] Thus, he explains the relationship between the Egyptian government and the Islamic rules on adultery, fornication, theft, and the like:

> These are rules that have been legislated by God, and they remain valid until the coming of The Hour. We cannot change them and we cannot expunge the verses that prescribe the punishment for adultery, fornication, or theft. However, where the government refuses to apply these rules for particular reasons, such as the fact that we are not alone in the world, or that there are other powers lying in wait for us, or out of fear that this will cause civil strife between Muslims

and Christians—under such circumstances, we accept the government's excuse and we say that the ruler is a Muslim, that he neither rejects *sharī'ah* nor attacks it but finds himself in circumstances that prevent him from applying it. And it is absolutely not permissible to brand such a ruler an Unbeliever.[106]

Of course, going all the way back to the days of 'Abd al-Salām Faraj and the coalition, a cardinal principle had been that Muslim governments that refuse or fail to apply *sharī'ah* deserve no recognition from believing Muslims and must be overthrown. Now, however, based on what it recognizes as *fiqh al-wāqi'* (reality-based jurisprudence), the *Gamā'ah* recognizes that the government *may* be justified in temporarily setting this or that particular rule aside. Moreover, based on its apparent recognition of the distinction between *law,* on the one hand, and *government* or *policy,* on the other, that is, between the hermeneutical interpretation-cum-reconciliation of *texts* and the factual assessment-cum-determination of *public interest,* the *Gamā'ah* is willing to cede to the Egyptian government substantial authority and powers of discretion regarding the latter. In other words, it is the government's and not the *Gamā'ah*'s assessment of the likely consequences of applying a law that is to be recognized, *ceteris paribus,* as dispositive.[107]

To be sure, placing jihad in this more "practical" context might cast it in a more benign light; but there are a number of disjunctive implications lurking in the background that could have serious boomerang effects. This is essentially the point raised by 'Abd al-Raḥīm 'Alī, a leftist detractor of the *Gamā'ah* who questioned the overall value of the Initiative, noting that, on the *Gamā'ah*'s logic, if their brand of bloody jihad *had* succeeded in promoting the Faith, this type of political violence would still be a religious obligation.[108]

Similarly, if the linchpin of the *Gamā'ah*'s abandonment of violence is its factual assessment of the likely consequences thereof, anyone who rejected *their* factual assessment could justify the most radical expressions of jihad based on their own assessment of its anticipated outcome. Of course, the *Gamā'ah* leadership is keenly aware of this liability. Rather than react, however, via an overindulgence of essentially circular counterargument, their response is basically to insist that, in their view, their erstwhile romantic notion of the panacean power of wanton, violent jihad simply presupposes the existence of a world fundamentally different from the one we now inhabit. In other words, the *Gamā'ah* sees their assessment of the implications and likely outcome of their former commitment to jihad as far less subjective than 'Alī is willing or perhaps able to recognize. For, in their view, *anyone* living in the modern world can observe the palpably diminishing role and long-term effectiveness of brute force and unbridled power in domestic or geopolitical contests, especially where the aim is to effect genuine change in ideology or conviction. This recognition on the *Gamā'ah*'s part can hardly be said, in other words, to be a unique perspective of theirs. Rather, in their view, it enjoys broad and increasing recognition across the globe.[109] To be sure, those who disagree with or reject this perspective may indeed subscribe to the logic adduced by 'Alī. But this should neither bind nor implicate the *Gamā'ah* nor overshadow the fact that the latter's newly adopted *fiqh al-wāqi'* simply moves in the opposite direction.

This new insight ultimately informs the ideational context in which the *Gamā'ah* leaders extend their analysis beyond Egypt to the modern world as a whole, bringing them to a critique of contemporary "jihadism" in general and of *al-Qā'idah* in particular. This is exhaustively laid out in a book they published in January

2004, *Al-Qāʿidah's Strategy and Bombings: Mistakes and Dangers* (*Istrātijīyah wa tafjīrāt al-Qāʿidah: al-Akhṭāʾ wa al-akhṭār*). Here they explicitly contrast what they refer to as the "vision of the Initiative" with the "vision of *al-Qāʿidah.*" Again, their basic critique is that *al-Qāʿidah* misunderstands the rules and purposes of jihad and ignores or misapprehends contemporary reality. This leads *al-Qāʿidah* to a misapplication of jihad and to consequences that actually undermine rather than promote its prescribed objective. To be sure, *Gamāʿah* leaders are careful to note that they mean no disrespect to "Shaykh" Usāmah b. Lādin, nor to impugn *al-Qāʿidah*'s intentions, nor to downplay America's negative role in the Muslim world. Their aim is simply to clarify the mistakes that have befallen *al-Qāʿidah*'s understanding of jihad, along with the harm that has accompanied this, based on an understanding of *sharīʿah* principles that they themselves have now come to recognize and espouse.[110]

According to the *Gamāʿah, al-Qāʿidah* basically misunderstands jihad on two levels. First, they tend to see it as an end in itself rather than a means to the end of promoting the efficacy of the Faith. While violence, according to the *Gamāʿah, might* play a role in this enterprise, this is a secondary, supportive role rather than a primary one; for, ultimately, violence cannot replace persuasion, the sine qua non of true faith. This, the *Gamāʿah* insists, is an oversight committed by many Muslims today. In fact, in a revisionist depiction of the Ottomans, they claim "they placed jihad over persuasion and guiding the people," which is why, they intimate, Islam never struck deep roots in much of Ottoman Europe.[111]

Second, in addition to its overestimation of jihad, *al-Qāʿidah* has an overinclusive understanding of its scope, by virtue of which it condones, for example, the killing of noncombatants, including innocent "civilians." Here the *Gamāʿah* begins with the claim that, with the exception of al-Imām al-Shāfiʿī, all of the classical schools of Islamic law hold non-Muslims' *aggression* against the Muslims and not their *unbelief* to be the reason that they can or should be fought. This is why the classical schools made exceptions for women, children, the elderly, monks, farmers, the blind, and so on, none of whom, in contradistinction to the generality of fighting-age men, could be assumed to be combatants. In fact, the majority of these exceptions even al-Imām al-Shāfiʿī accepts. Now, as far as the *Gamāʿah* is concerned, these exceptions are the functional equivalent of modern "civilians," who, like their medieval analogs, are not to be fought, because they play no direct role and pose no direct threat in any actual fighting.[112] Beyond this, the *Gamāʿah* leaders draw a subtle but interesting distinction between *categories* of persons that can be fought and *individual members* of these categories who can be killed. They point out, for example, that while a Muslim ruler can fight rebels as a group and of course kill them in the course of this fighting, he cannot, at least according to most jurists, kill *individual* rebels once they have been subdued and cease to pose a physical threat to the sociopolitical order.[113] Aggression, in other words, may be a legitimate basis for identifying a group *in general* as an enemy and taking measures to beat back their aggression. This is not the same, however, as identifying every *individual member* of that group as an enemy to be killed or attacked at will, unless the latter actually poses a direct threat or engages in or contributes to his or her group's actual aggression.[114] To quote the *Gamāʿah,* "even if *al-Qāʿidah* deems it a religious duty to *fight* against America, this does not mean that it is permissible to *kill any* and all American civilians anywhere in the world."[115]

All of this is set against the backdrop of the *Gamāʿah*'s third main critique of *al-Qāʿidah,* namely its obliviousness to or faulty assessment of contemporary reality, most particularly regarding the role, agenda, and influence of the United States. Specifically, the *Gamā'ah* sees *al-Qā'idah* as being driven by ideological commitments that blind it to important historical facts and prevent it from seeing the connection, or the lack thereof, between these facts, its actions, and its purported goals. For example—and this list is not exhaustive—*al-Qā'idah* sees America as leading an international conspiracy to wipe out Islam; it deems U.S. and Muslim interests to be mutually and permanently contradictory; thus, it holds any kind of truce, negotiation, or alliance with America to be tantamount to Islamic treason.

The *Gamā'ah*'s response is, first of all, to argue that any international conspiracy against Islam as might exist only came about *after* 9/11. As such, *al-Qā'idah* itself must take much of the responsibility for this alleged fact. Second, and this is also related to the first point, while U.S.-Muslim world interests *may* clash in *some* times and places, history clearly proves that this is not the case in *all* times and places. As an example, the *Gamā'ah* holds up U.S. support for the *Mujāhidīn* in Afghanistan against the Soviet Union. Finally, the *Gamā'ah* notes, the notion that jihad is the only acceptable response to modern geopolitical reality and that contracting truces, treaties, and alliances with America is an act of Islamic treason simply contradicts well-known practices of the Prophet himself, who, for example, made peace treaties with non-Muslim Arabians who opposed, vilified, and attacked him and his religion. Similarly, he entered into alliances with the Jews and pagans of Medina in a pact to defend the city from outside attack and preserve its internal peace and security *for all.*[116]

Again, none of this should be taken to indicate *Gamā'ah*'s approval of America's negative or imperial role in the region. They repeatedly point to America's bias vis-à-vis the Arab-Israeli conflict, its hypocritical, self-serving promotion of democracy, human rights,[117] and the protection of religious minorities and women, not to mention U.S. economic exploits and ambitions in the region. In the face of all of this, the *Gamā'ah*'s message is emphatically not one of "grin and bear it." It is simply to question the effectiveness, from the standpoint of reality, and the validity, from the standpoint of *sharī'ah,* of the kind of wanton violence and bellicosity advocated by *al-Qā'idah.* For, if the overall aim of this "jihadism" is—as it must be from the standpoint of the religious law—to promote the interests of Islam, not only has it not done this, it has gone so far as to turn the entire world not only against *al-Qā'idah* but against Islam as a whole.[118]

Of course, even in the United States there are those who openly express the view that America has squandered her good name across the globe and come to be viewed more as a self-serving imperial dictator than a global servant or bearer of good. It is in this context that *Gamā'ah* leaders cite a rhetorical question from an Islamist who asks why Muslims should *not* unleash a religious war against America and the West, in order to awaken the Muslim Community from its slumber and humiliation, raise its spirit, and resolve to stop these Western conspiracies in their tracks. To this the *Gamā'ah* responds:

> We disagree with this logic, not only because the Ummah is ill-prepared to make such a choice but also because we think that awakening the Ummah from its slumber and helping it resume its role as a contributor to human civilization requires that we not fall into the trap of a clash of civilizations [*ṣadām al-ḥaḍārāt*]. Rather, this requires a policy of civilizational dia-

logue [tawāṣul al-ḥaḍārāt] while preserving our Islamic identity and defending ourselves and waging jihad against any aggression against our religion's fundamental constitution or our vital religious, national or international interests.[119]

In the *Gamā'ah*'s view, *al-Qā'idah* (like this questioner) tends to see jihad (i.e., as armed confrontation) as the singular response to the challenge of America and the West. Moreover, *al-Qā'idah* seems confident that success in this regard, that is, on the battlefield, will be sufficient to promote and preserve the interests of Islam. The *Gamā'ah*, by contrast, neither sees jihad as the only response nor military victory as a panacea.[120] For it understands the interests of Islam to go beyond the mere accumulation and exercise of power. And it is unwilling to allow the ostensibly unqualified duty to engage in jihad to outstrip or undermine the broader aims and objectives of the religion itself, chief among these being, again, to connect people to their Lord and direct them to the path of God. This is the context in which we might best understand the response of Ḥamdī 'Abd al-Raḥmān, when asked about the difference between the *Gamā'ah* and *al-Qā'idah*. He responded: "It is the difference between us today and us in the past. *Al-Qā'idah* still privileges (individual) texts over the broader aims and objectives of Islam."[121]

Secondary Arguments: The Problem of the Coptic Minority

The Egyptian state was not the only object of *Gamā'ah* violence. Bloody hostilities with Coptic Christians were also a major catalyst in these confrontations. Having relied, however, on specifically *sharīʿah*-based principles to guide them away from wanton jihad, the issue of the Copts remained outstanding. This was particularly problematic given that the *sharīʿah*-tradition from which the Initiative to Stop the Violence so heavily drew assigned Jews and Christians, as "People of the Book" (*Ahl al-Kitāb*), a place in a normatively operating Muslim polity—now the Islamic state—that modern, democratically oriented Copts (or other religious minorities) might reasonably be assumed to reject. Specifically, Islamic law traditionally required non-Muslim minorities to pay a special religious tax, the so-called *jizya,* in exchange for their right to exist, practice their religion, avoid military service and enjoy state-sponsored protection. Given the "*sharīʿah*-based approach" undergirding the Initiative, the *Gamāʿah* had now to come to terms with this traditionally recognized feature of the religious law, if they were to avoid agitation among their Coptic compatriots and insulate their efforts from backsliding toward at least one iteration of the violence of the past.

This issue is explicitly addressed during the course of their discussion of the eighth of the aforementioned series of "legal impediments" laid out in *Initiative to Stop the Violence,* which they designate as "pertaining specifically to the People of the Book." After rehearsing the traditional position that renders religious minorities inviolable upon their agreement to pay the *jizya,* they go directly to the problem: "Now, if it is said: But in our times, when states neither demand of the People of the Book living in their jurisdictions that they pay any tax on religious minorities nor extend to them any contracts of protection, what should the relationship be between the Islamist movements and the People of the Book? Should they fight them until they agree to pay the tax on religious minorities? Or should they simply leave them alone or what?"[122]

The *Gamāʿah*'s response is essentially that exacting the *jizya* is the exclusive preserve of the state, which substate groups and individuals have neither the right nor responsibility to undertake. The main reason for this, they point out, is that this tax entails reciprocal obligations, such as the guarantee of security, which substate groups and individuals have no ability to fulfill. This leads ultimately to the conclusion that they, as merely an Islamic *movement,* do not have the authority to exact the *jizya.* As for the Egyptian state, as in the case of the religious law in general, as we have seen, they will not second-guess its decision to apply or not to apply this (or other) particular provision(s) of *sharīʿah.* Of course, if the aim here is to assure Coptic Christians of their nonexposure to this tax in the kind of modern Islamic state that the *Gamāʿah* ultimately remains committed to establishing, these would appear to be palpably weak fortifications.[123] To be fair, however, the issue itself is not central to the *Gamāʿah*'s main argument (which is against political violence), as evidenced by the very brevity of the treatment it receives in the text. Still, the matter remains clearly unresolved, and this inadequate handling will almost certainly detract more from than it adds to any confidence the *Gamāʿah* might hope to inspire among Coptic Christians.[124]

And All the Victims?

As we have seen, *Gamāʿah* activities took an enormous toll on Egyptian society. While *Mubādarat waqf al-ʿunf* signals a general awareness of the damage to Egypt's stature and geopolitical effectiveness, it is not as forthcoming in its display of actual remorse, not to mention any desire to indemnify or even apologize to the families of the victims. At first blush, this might cast a cloud of suspicion if not opprobrium over the Initiative, as a cold and calculating attempt to restore the group's Islamist bona fides, while showing no more consideration for those who fell to their violence than absolutely necessary on either tactical or rhetorical grounds. To be fair, thematically speaking, this particular concern fell outside the primary aim of the text, which was to marshal specifically legal, that is, *sharī'ah*-based, arguments to legitimate the *Gamā'ah*'s Initiative against political violence among its own rank-and-file and to steer other radical jihadists away from the group's former approach. In this capacity, given the make-up and sensibilities of their audience, not to mention the government's desire to exploit the Initiative to its own advantage, it is easy to imagine how the need to sustain a show of strength and imperviousness to any form of pressure-driven compromise might crowd out any room for too ready a display of empathy or contrition.

Yet, further away from these more immediate constraints and pressures, the *Gamā'ah* openly acknowledged and lamented the suffering and dislocation they had inflicted upon their compatriots, even going so far as to express a will to make amends. During one of his exchanges with the group, Makram Muḥammad Aḥmad asks them pointedly, "Are you prepared to offer an apology to the Egyptian people for the misdeeds and crimes that you have committed against them?"[125] To this, Karam Zuhdī, the uncontested leader of the *Gamā'ah,* responds: "We have done this in all of our sessions in the prisons: we have announced the mistake we made in deciding on violent confrontation in the 1990s. And I hereby reaffirm that we owe the Egyptian people an apology for the crimes committed by *al-Gamā'ah al-Islāmīyah* against Egypt. But we will not only tender an apology; we have thought seriously within the Consultative Council about giving blood money [*dīyah*] to the families of the victims of the events of the past, from the proceeds of our books, if we are able and God grants us the resources to do so."[126]

Again, given its acute ideational, tactical, and sociopolitical context, much of this comes through only implicitly in *Initiative to Stop the Violence.* In the broader, more general context of their post-Initiative regrouping, however, the new *Gamā'ah* clearly expressed remorse and perhaps even an element of shame for the pain and suffering they had visited upon their beloved Egypt.

Implications

The *Gamā'ah*'s Initiative to Stop the Violence remains the oldest and, by most accounts, the most serious reform effort among contemporary radical jihadist movements. In particular, the group has been noted for its willingness to engage in principled self-critique and to ground its arguments in the sources and tradition of Islam in a manner suggestive of genuine ideological change, not to mention the ability to endure external criticism and sustain the needed multiplier effect over time. To date (2014), more than a decade has passed on the group's public issuance of its manifestos, and the Initiative itself is more than a decade and a half old. The *Gamā'ah* has not committed, sponsored, supported, or condoned any major acts of political violence since it announced this change, clearly turning its back on its radical jihadist ideology and the "jurisprudence of violence" that underwrote it. In his study, Omar Ashour notes that, since the *Gamā'ah* launched its initiative, other radical jihadist groups, in and outside of Egypt, have followed suit with "deradicalization programs of their own."[127] Indeed, the *Gamā'ah* itself claims that other radical groups appealed to them while they were still in prison to assist them in getting their reform efforts off the ground.[128] Chief among these were their former "rivals," Jihad Inc., as reflected in the corrective manifesto written by its notorious former leader, Sayyid Imām (Dr. Faḍl), *A Document for the Guidance of Jihadi Missions in Egypt and the World* (*Wathīqat tarshīd al-'amal al-jihādī fī miṣr wa al-'ālam*), which appeared in 2007.[129]

All of this raises the question, of course, of the likely impact of the *Gamā'ah*'s Initiative and corrective manifestos on the future of radical jihadism overall. Here I am inclined to agree with the suggestion of 'Abd al-Mun'im Munīb, who doubts that the *Gamā'ah*'s effort will lead to any across-the-board renunciation of political violence by groups who are already committed to such. But, as he also notes, the *Gamā'ah*'s effort has clearly instigated a new conversation both on and within radical jihadism.[130] And given their unimpeachable Islamist bona fides and street credibility, their reformist articulations will almost certainly complicate efforts by other young, radical jihadists to infuse their rhetoric with the insinuation that only "sell-outs," hypocrites, or those who are lukewarm or soft in their commitment to Islam or the establishment of an Islamic state could possibly object to their understanding or advocacy of jihad as holy terror. To this should be added the cumulative impact on older activists who at one point or another either opposed or nursed misgivings about the *Gamā'ah*'s reforms. Take, for example, Ṭāriq al-Zumar, who played a crucial role in bringing the coalition together back in the 1980s and spent decades in prison as a result. He initially opposed the Initiative and, even after leaving Jihad Inc. and joining the *Gamāʿah* in 1991, being immediately inducted into the Consultative Council, he never signed any of the manifestos issued in the group's name. Yet, not only would he eventually come to endorse the Initiative, he would explicitly come to recognize "nonviolence" (*al-ʿamal al-silmī*) as the greatest source of "Islam's strategic power and among the most important means of advancing the Islamic awakening"![131]

This brings me to the following closing thoughts. As the text under review, *Initiative to Stop the Violence,* clearly demonstrates, the Historical Leadership thoroughly familiarized themselves with the traditional Islamic religious sciences during their tenure in prison. It is also clear, however, that this alone was not the key to their success. As far back as the 1980s and especially the early 1990s, there had been attempts by such luminaries as the Rector of al-Azhar, the grand Mufti of Egypt, Shaykh Muḥammad al-Ghazālī, Shaykh Muḥammad Mutawallī al-Shaʿrāwī, and other nonclerics, for example, Fahmī Huwaydī, to disabuse radical jihadists of their "jurisprudence of violence" and/or broker a cease-fire.[132] All of these efforts failed. Yet, in their vindication of their Initiative to Stop the Violence, the *Gamāʿah* drew on a conspicuously *traditional* set of arguments—indeed, to a large extent, an emphatically traditional universe of meanings, tropes, and articulations—on which these religious figures would seem to have much greater purchase. This, I think, should alert us to at least three things.

First, religious authority in contemporary Islam is not the exclusive preserve of those commonly identified as the guardians of the classical tradition. Rather, besides mastery of tradition, which is clearly the sine qua non of *formal* religious authority, other qualities or associations—for example, a "heroic stance" or, if you will, "street credibility"—may be equally or even more constitutive of *informal* religious authority, depending on the audience. While, generally speaking, the avenues to mastering tradition remain clear and formally regulated (e.g., through the granting of degrees and formal authorizations to issue *fatwā*s), access to this "secondary," informal authority remains open and up for grabs.[133] For radical jihadists (or perhaps even others) the *Gamā'ah* and its leadership simply have more of this informal authority than do their formally trained (and other) counterparts. As such, they are likely to be far more effective in reaching these types of audiences (and maybe even others). In such light, perhaps their contributions to resolving some of the problems or realizing some of the possibilities confronting Islam and Muslims in the modern world, including East-West relations, should neither be automatically assessed as negative nor summarily dismissed as inconsequential.

Second, the categories through which we have grown accustomed to anticipating or even demanding critical Muslim responses to wanton violence committed in the name of Islam may call for reassessment. As the *Gamā'ah*'s Initiative clearly demonstrates, "moderates"—or those we tend to think of or identify as moderates—are not the only ones whose ideological commitments can sustain or even compel principled condemnations of promiscuous, political violence. Rather, *sharī'ah* itself, whether as presided over by traditional clergy, or as adopted and deployed by those who come to that tradition from "without"—including bearded so-called "fundamentalists"—can also be invoked and mobilized against capricious killing in the name of Islam. On this recognition, it may be time to reexamine if not discard the notion, often more implied than explicitly stated, that "Westernization," reduced religiosity, or secularization are the only or most effective means of promoting peaceful conflict resolution with or among Muslims.

Finally, texts alone are not autonomously self-determinative of the uses to which they are put. The same Qur'ān, Sunna, and writings of Ibn Taymīya that were deployed by 'Abd al-Salām Faraj in his incendiary *The Neglected Duty* (*al-Farīḍah al-ghā'ibah*) were deployed by the *Gamā'ah*'s Historical Leadership in promoting and vindicating their Initiative to Stop the Violence. Clearly, in such light, to continue to assign independent, determinative agency to ancient religious texts or authorities, as if existential circumstances—repression, humiliation, prison, occupation, civilizational domination, or intellectual maturation—contribute nothing to the ways in which these are read and pressed into service, is to fall victim to the strictures of one's own ideological prism, ultimately resulting in what might amount to a form of "reverse fundamentalism," or in Amitai Etzioni's words, a species of "Multiple Realism Deficiency Disorder."[134]

The Text and Translation

My translation is based on the first, original edition of this text. I have altered the paragraphing on occasion to facilitate greater flow and coherence in English. And I have ignored minor mistakes in the original (e.g., missing or extra diacritics). Also, the original text includes numerous footnotes. These are represented in the translation by numbered endnotes. Where I saw fit to add an explanatory note, I placed it between square brackets, either in sequence with the authors' notes or simply appended to one of them. Unfortunately, the authors do not provide information on the editions, publishers or dates of publication of the texts they adduce. As such, I have not been able to provide this information, as there are literally dozens of editions of some of the texts they cite (for example, the *Ṣaḥīḥ* collections of Muslim and al-Bukhārī). This drastically reduces the utility of the numbers they provide as references to hadith in these works.

I provide the death-dates of all scholars (excluding Companions and other early sources of hadith) cited in the text, in order to give a clearer sense of the vast and random chronological expanse covered by the *Gamāʿah*'s appropriations. Repeated panegyric optatives are rather cumbersome in English. As such, I use the symbol "*" for "*ṣubḥānahu wa taʿālā* (be He praised and exalted), and the like, after the mention of God. I use "•" for *ṣalla Allāhu ʿalayhi wa sallama* (God's blessings and salutations be upon him), and the like, following the mention of the Prophet Muḥammad or any other prophet. And I use "°" for *raḍiya Allāhu ʿanhu* (may God be pleased with him) and *raḥimahu Allāh* (may God have mercy on him) after the mention of a Companion or any later Muslim figure, respectively.

One vocabulary item in the translation calls perhaps for specific comment. This is the *Gamāʿah*'s use of the Arabic word, *al-shāriʿ*, which I translate as "Lawgiver." On its face, *al-shāriʿ* in Arabic can refer to God, the Prophet, or even, depending on context, a modern legislature. As used by the *Gamāʿah,* however, it applies exclusively to God, and then by extension the Prophet, as God's representative. The *Gamāʿah* never uses this term in this text to refer, for example, to the head of a premodern or modern Muslim state, a state legislature, the community of Muslim jurists (*al-fuqahāʾ*), or any other earthly individual or institution. Indeed, from their perspective, to view as "Lawgiver" (in any ultimate sense) anyone other than God or His Messenger would be to violate Islamic monotheism (*tawḥīd*).

I have tried to be true to the substance, spirit, and tone of the *Gamāʿah*'s manifesto. In this regard, I have tried to convey their meanings in the fullness of the "supercontext" of the classical tradition from which they draw, even as it flows into, is refracted by, and ultimately attenuated through the modern experience. In this context, rather than burden my reader with an unending plethora of brackets, given the highly elliptical nature of classical Arabic, I have tried to keep these to a minimum, though I have obviously found it necessary to read my own understanding into the elliptical nooks and crannies of the text. I use rounded brackets either to confirm the use of an Arabic technical term in the original, or where the appropriateness of my interpolations seem obvious but might raise minor questions. Where the appropriateness of my interpolations are less obvious, I use square brackets. In the latter part of the translation, I use pointed brackets to represent material that is bracketed in the original text, where the authors draw on supercommentaries that include original works and their commentaries. In the end, as always, I can only hope, and this is my solemn prayer, that in my effort to introduce this text to the English-speaking world, my pen did not get the better of me and I have compromised neither myself nor the courageous effort of the Historical Leadership of *al-Gamāʿah al-Islāmīyah.*

Initiative to Stop the Violence

A Reality-Based Assessment and a *Sharī'ah*-Based Approach

Introduction

1 Indeed, all praise is due God. We praise Him, seek His aid, and ask for His forgiveness. We seek refuge in God from the evil that lurks within ourselves and from the wickedness that inevitably befalls our deeds. Whomever God guides, none can lead astray. And whomever God leads astray,[1] none can guide. I bear witness that there is no god except God, Who is one and has no partner. And I bear witness that Muḥammad is His servant and His messenger. *O you who believe, be conscious of God as fully as you ought, and die not unless you are in a state of submission to God* [3:102]. *O people, be*

conscious of your Lord Who created you from a single soul and from it created its mate and brought forth men and women in multitudes. Be conscious of your Lord about whom you shall be asked, along with the wombs (that brought you forth). Verily God is in watching over you [4:1]. *O you who believe, be conscious of God, and speak words of directness. He will set right your deeds and forgive your sins. And whoever obeys God and His messenger achieves a mighty triumph indeed* [33:70].

2 To proceed: The most truthful speech is the word of God*. And the best model is the model of Muhammad•. The worse undertakings are those that defy established precedent. And every undertaking that defies established precedent is an unsanctioned innovation. Every unsanctioned innovation is misguidance. And every form of misguidance is destined for Hell.

3 On July 5, 1997, during a review of military case number 235, all in attendance were stunned by one of the defendants, who stood up, faced the members of the press, and read aloud a proclamation, to which was appended the signatures of the Historical Leadership of al-*Gamā'ah al-Islāmīyah,* in which they called upon the membership to halt all armed operations and to desist from bloodshed. This "surprise," as they say, was like a rock cast into a pool of standing water, to be quickly followed by a successive stream of ripple effects: some hastened to dismiss this gesture and to cast doubts and aspersions upon it; others took a more staid approach of waiting to see what the coming days would bring, refraining from expressing either support or opposition. Most, however, hastened to support this development, applauding and encouraging it, in hopes that this courageous Initiative might be a portal through which the country might escape the bloodbath through which it had suffered for so many years.

4 Though this Initiative had come of the unilateral efforts of one side only, the state apparatus evincing no positive response other than to foster an atmosphere of optimism that the crisis at hand might be finally put to rest, many people suspected that everyone would eventually come around. This feeling of optimism increased when our shaykh, Dr. 'Umar 'Abd al-Raḥmān, hastened, from his jail cell in America—may God unfetter his shackles—to support this move and called upon all of the brothers to go along with it. As for our brethren abroad, they (initially) announced their unwillingness to go along with this Initiative, even expressing doubts about whether it had actually issued from us. Meanwhile, the difficulties in communicating with them from prison posed barriers that greatly impeded our ability to explain our point of view, even though we were confident at the time that things would eventually end in their approval.

5 Then, in the throws of our efforts to find ways to explain our point of view to our brethren, as mutual recriminations regarding the Initiative raged among the general public and the state apparatus alike, we were blindsided by the Luxor massacre. This was a shock to us all, especially since it included violations of women and children and the mutilation of their bodies, all of which was alien to our approach and ideology. This atrocity reverberated widely, however, with disparate effects.

6 Nevertheless, we persisted in affirming our commitment to our Initiative, despite a sense of demoralization that had begun to creep into our souls. At the same time, this incident resonated negatively in the souls of our brethren abroad, and their endorsements began to file in, one after another, until finally they announced their own joint proclamation on March 28, 1999, in which they expressed full support and agreed to halt all armed operations along with

all proclamations encouraging such. The Initiative became, thus, a threshold upon which all the members of the *Gamā'ah* gathered in hopes that they would be able to throw off the effects of the dark days of the past in order to be able to return to their original mission as callers to God who contribute to guiding people to God's straight path. Four years have now passed on the announcement of the Initiative, and we continue to enjoy a sense of relief, as we watch the tree of our Initiative gradually blossom.

7 Armed operations have ceased. The flow of blood has stopped. And the climate has become more amenable to arriving at a solution to that most intractable of problems, which brought about all these tragic events to begin with: the plight of the incarcerated! One could now begin to look to a future that was brighter and characterized by greater awareness. And the voices of the doubt sowers began to fade, as they watched the days pass and increasingly confirm our sincerity and commitment to fulfilling the pledges that we had taken upon ourselves, despite the trials, setbacks, and pressures to which the Initiative had been subjected. In fact, time would confirm that we were the most committed of people to restoring our luminous missionary profile, which had suffered such disfiguration over the past several years.

8 Still, some of our brethren continued to ask: "Does this Initiative conceal some kind of backroom deal, in which we seek to retrieve some worldly advantage in exchange for which we agree to relinquish our commitment to calling people to God? And, what are the *sharī'ah*-based proofs to validate this Initiative?"

9 Thus, to our brethren who have disappeared behind the walls of prison, veiled from the world and denied the opportunity to meet and exchange ideas; and to our brethren on the outside from

whose presence we have disappeared behind the walls of prison, which have prevented us from being able to inform them (directly) of our true intentions and ideological perspective, even if all of them have responded positively to our efforts on a basic emotional and intellectual level; and to all others who ask along with them the same basic questions they ask, we say the following.

10 This Initiative, which we have launched, is not a compromise in which we trade our religion for some fleeting worldly advantage. Nor is it a compromise that oscillates between striving to gain public recognition for the religion of God and His Sacred Law and some cheap worldly gain, concern for which we have long thrown behind our backs. Rather this Initiative is grounded in our understanding that the violent position we use to assume is one that the luminous *sharīʿah* simply forbids, due to its greatly harmful effects. And (clarifying) this fact is a religious obligation, the fulfillment of which we have taken upon ourselves, with all due courageousness. None of this, however, contradicts another obligation to which we all are bound: striving to elevate the religion of God and establishing His *sharīʿah.* In this light, terminating (our erstwhile) political violence constitutes a religious obligation. So does calling people to establish the Law of God and propagating His religion. Indeed, we must rise to fulfill both of these obligations.

11 To proceed: Let us thus begin our discussion with all of you with the proofs and correctly understood concepts that led us to announce this Initiative. All of these are derived from our unencumbered Sacred Law. And though, given our particular circumstances, this discussion will necessarily be brief, we believe that it will be sufficient. And we ask God to guide us along the straight path.

Chapter One: The Commonweal and Communal Harm

12 Promoting the commonweal, as the great al-Shāṭibī (d. 790/1388) put it, "is *the* foundational principle of the *sharī'ah*. For the *sharī'ah* was simply sent down to promote the religious and secular commonweal of humans and to divert communal harm away from them." This understanding finds indubitable confirmation in the broader aims and objectives of the Wise Lawgiver, as manifested in His revelation. And rational and other textual proofs also converge on this meaning. Here, however, we will simply cite some of the Qur'ānic verses and Prophetic examples that throw this understanding into relief, as the aggregate of proofs that support this position are so expansive and numerous that they defy quantification.

13 God* says: *They ask you about wine-drinking and games of chance. Say, in them is great vice, along with benefits for people; but their vice is greater than their benefit* [2:219]. This verse, as noted by Shaykh al-Islam Ibn Taymīya (d. 728/1328), tied the prohibition on wine drinking and games of chance to the fact that the harm known to attach to them is greater than the benefit they promote. In other words, the great vice represented by the obliteration of the rational faculties and the emergence, as a result, of behaviors that go unsupervised by the faculty of reason is much greater than the benefit of the pleasure and rapture that accompanies wine drinking. For this reason, wine drinking, along with games of chance, have been forbidden.

14 Similarly, God* says, *Do not curse those to whom they supplicate other than God, lest they should curse God, as an unmindful act of retaliation* [6:108]. This verse prohibited cursing and denigrating the gods of the pagan polytheists so that the pagan polytheists would not curse God*, though such cursing and denigration would un-

doubtedly constitute a prima facie benefit, inasmuch as they would discourage people from worshipping such gods. In other words, the harm contained in their potentially cursing God* was greater than any benefit that might attach to cursing and obviating the deficiencies of the pagan polytheists' gods or of attempting to mount a proselytizing campaign based on such a critique. For this reason these actions were forbidden.

15 Al-Qurṭubī (d. 671/1272) said: "In this is proof that a person who is entitled to a right may forego that right—though obtaining one's right is undoubtedly a benefit—if pursuing such a right is likely to result in a comparatively greater harm to his or her religion." Ibn Kathīr (d. 774/1373) said: "God* spoke the aforementioned verse, prohibiting His Prophet• and the believers from cursing the gods of the pagan polytheists, even though there is benefit in such cursing, except that this benefit entails a greater harm, which is the pagan polytheists' reciprocating by cursing the god of the believers." Ibn Kathīr added: "And of this category, that is, abandoning a benefit in order to avoid a greater harm, is what appears in the *Ṣaḥīḥ* collections (of al-Bukhārī and Muslim) where the Prophet• said, 'Indeed, among the greatest of grave sins is for a man to curse his parents.' It was said, 'O Messenger of God, how can a man curse his parents?' He responded, 'A man curses the father of another man, as a result of which the latter curses the former's father. Or he curses the latter's mother, as a result of which the latter curses his mother.'"[2]

16 Let us look as well at the example of the Prophet himself• in his recognition that the Ka'ba had been rebuilt on foundations other than those laid down by Abraham•. Prior to Islam, the people of Mecca had rebuilt the Ka'ba following a flood that destroyed it. But they ran short of money and were unable to reestablish it

on Abraham's foundations. So they rebuilt it to narrower dimensions. The Prophet,• however, refrained from dismantling and then rebuilding it (on Abraham's foundations) because he recognized that the people of Mecca were quite new in the religion and that such an action might unduly try them in their faith. Thus he• said to 'Ā'ishah,° "Were it not that your people were so recently emergent from their pre-Islamic state, I would order the Sacred House to be dismantled and restore to it what had been taken from it."[3] Thus, he took the strife that would have resulted from dismantling and rebuilding the Sacred House—such strife undoubtedly constituting a clear harm—as an impediment to rebuilding it on its proper foundations upon which it should have been built. And this was the interest that this hadith aimed to capture.

17 Observe him• also, as he praises the "Sword of Islam," Khālid b. al-Walīd, when the latter returned from the campaign against Mu'tah, having withdrawn the Muslim army without achieving victory. The Prophet described this army as "oft-attackers," despite the fact that the youth of Medina had gathered and begun to pelt some of the men of this unit with rocks and earth, shouting, "Runaways! You fled from the path of God."[4] This retreating army numbered no more than three thousand fighters, whereas the Byzantines numbered two hundred thousand! The battle between the two armies had gone on all day, and the three generals who led the Muslim army had all fallen. To persist under such circumstances would have meant the complete annihilation of the Muslim army, not to mention the certain demise of that paltry unit, with all that that would have entailed in the way of a deeply negative blow to the morale of the young Muslim state. Without doubt, saving the army from this slaughter was a great benefit, even as appearing to retreat in defeat was a reprehensible evil. But the great leader

masterfully assessed the situation and accorded precedence to the benefit of retreating and saving his small army. Thus, the Prophet• praised him and referred to him in this battle as the "Sword of God," describing his action as a victory. Indeed, he• said, "Then one of 'God's swords' took the flag and God brought victory through him."[5]

18 Yes, it was a victory without doubt, the fact of retreating notwithstanding. For the Sword of God understood that the Lawgiver's aim in prescribing jihad was not merely to spill blood and be overtaken by death. Rather, it was to realize a goal beyond fighting, which is to elevate the word of God and spread His religion. Undoubtedly, however, this goal would not be realized were the Muslim army annihilated. Indeed, jihad is not a goal in and of itself. On the contrary, it must serve some preponderant benefit beyond itself. And whenever that benefit ceases to exist, there ceases to be any point in continuing to fight. Rather, fighting becomes an evil that must be eschewed.

19 Also, among the applications of this principle of promoting the commonweal is what the Commander of the Faithful 'Umar b. al-Khaṭṭāb° did when he forbade the distribution of frontier lands to the victorious Muslim conquerors. Frontier lands are those that are captured by Muslims through war, which are then divided into fifths and distributed, alongside the spoils, according to the rules of *sharī'ah*. But 'Umar ordered that these lands remain in the hands of their original owners from among the inhabitants of the conquered territories, settling for the imposition of a land tax upon them, as he deemed it a greater benefit for the original inhabitants, who were more knowledgeable about the upkeep of these lands, to tend to them, given the soldiery's preoccupation with war. In other words, the interest of having the original owners care for these

lands was greater than the interest of distributing them among the Muslims, since the latter option would entail taking the soldiery out of commission, by dint of their preoccupation with the land.

20 Another application of the principle is the jurists' prohibiting judges from passing rulings based on their own personal knowledge of the facts of a case, despite the fact that such knowledge might be more reliable than the testimony of witnesses. Indeed, when corruption and undisciplined passions became rife, the interest of litigants and of justice came to reside in tying all rulings to formal courtroom evidence, instead of relying on the judge's individual conscience.

21 In a similar fashion, many jurists forbid the implementation of the prescribed criminal punishments in predominantly non-Muslim lands where Muslims do not enjoy security, out of fear of the harm that will result from convicted criminals joining the enemy in order to escape punishment. In other words, they give precedence to the interest of preserving the physical integrity of the Community over the interest of the deterrence sought through criminal sanctions. Similarly, when the jurists saw how corruption had spread among the people, they made joint proprietary hirelings legally liable for damages, in violation of the rules governing service-leases, according to which hirelings are not legally liable.

22 Let us look as well at the Companions of the Prophet•, he having bequeathed the Qur'ān to them uncollated in their hearts and personal notes. They in turn assessed the commonweal to reside in collecting and collating it and gathering the people upon a single text, burning everything besides this official codex. This plan was implemented, and they destroyed the various notes that people had in their possession, in the interest of protecting the text of the Qur'ān from corruption. The people were thus gathered

upon a single codex whose collection they authenticated by means of diffusely congruent narration.

23 Let us also observe them as they arranged their nascent state. They established the caliphate, set up registries, built infrastructure, organized a court system and notarized agreements—none of this being based on any model that goes back to the time of the Prophet, there being no *sharīʿah*-based justification for this, save the promotion of the commonweal. And in this regard, the jurists have said, "Wherever we find the commonweal of the Muslims, we find the Sacred Law of God." And in this same context, it has been said, "What the Muslim community deems to be good is good in the sight of God."[6]

24 Indeed, many of the contracts that have been deemed legal or are explicitly endorsed by traditional authorities are actually in violation of the general rules governing contracts. And the reason for this is simply that the commonweal dictates the allowance of such contracts. For example, *ʿarāyah*-contracts violate the general rule banning *ribā*-interest.[7] Similarly, rentals (*ijārah*) and forward sales (*salam*) contain inevitable elements of proscribed uncertainty (*gharar*).[8] And these kinds of exceptions are numerous. Thus it is that the Wise Lawgiver routinely identifies general communal interests, as we have seen in the aforementioned texts, then leaves the scholars to concretize these in light of *sharīʿah*-based proofs and the broader aims and objectives of the *sharīʿah*, in accordance with stipulations that the legal theoreticians have spelled out with meticulous care. And they refer to such interests as "implicit interests" (*maṣlaḥah mursalah*).[9]

25 Now, given the importance of assessing interests and harms in guiding the deliberations of the scholars, establishing the rules of *sharīʿah*, guiding the actions and conduct of everyday Muslims and

subjecting these to relevant *sharī'ah*-based criteria, we will quickly allude to some of the most important principles governing this matter, which we present in the context of an assessment of the violence that raged between some of the youth belonging to various Islamic movements and the state apparatus, such violence routinely resulting in loss of life. We do this in an attempt to redirect these actions to their proper, *sharī'ah*-based ends.

26 The commonweal (*maṣlaḥah*) is the preservation of the desired aim of the Lawgiver, as the "Proof of Islam," Imām al-Ghazālī (d. 505/1111) defined it in his book *al-Mustaṣfā.* He went on to specify that the Lawgiver's desired aim for humanity is the preservation of five "vital necessities": (1) religion; (2) life; (3) the rational faculties; (4) progeny; and (5) property. Then he mentioned that anything that causes the forfeiture of these five fundamentals, or any one of them, is a harm and that the avoidance of such harm is a legitimate interest.

27 Now, the legal theoreticians also talk about another type of interest, which they call "valued interests."[10] These are interests the absence of whose realization does not throw life into complete disarray, as is the case with vital interests. Rather, their absence simply subjects life to hardship, difficulty, and undue constriction.

28 They go on, however, to speak of yet a third type, which they call "supplementary interests."[11] These are interests without the realization of which life is emptied of the higher moral affections, along with the lineaments of beauty and luxury. And many jurists, for example, Imām al-Ghazālī, lay down three stipulations for considering such implicit interests.

29 First: the implicit interest must be absolutely realizable, or at least it must be preponderant in one's thinking that it will be realized. There is no consideration to be given to suppositious interests or those whose realization is doubtful. Rather, the benefit

to be derived must be certain and free of doubt, or the harm to be avoided via its pursuit must be certain. They give as an example of this the collection of the Qur'ān after the death of the Prophet•, in the face of the deaths of growing numbers of people who had memorized the Qur'ān by heart.[12]

30 Second: the implicit interest must be a vital interest. Legal rulings cannot be negotiated on the basis of valued or supplementary interests that the Lawgiver did not explicitly identify.[13]

31 Third: the implicit interest must be universal and general in scope, covering the generality of people or at least most of them. By contrast, private interests are those whose benefit redounds upon a single party or class of people or some members of particular groups.

32 The *sharī'ah,* as "Shaykh al-Islam" Ibn Taymīya says, "came for the purpose of promoting the commonweal and bringing this to completion, as well as averting or limiting harm, giving consideration to the best of what is good and the least of what is evil."[14] Thus, the *sharī'ah* will seek to promote a greater interest at the expense of forfeiting a lesser one and to avert a greater harm at the expense of tolerating a lesser one.

33 Ibn Taymīya° goes on to add: "It becomes clear, then, that evil may be tolerated under two conditions: (1) where doing so averts a greater evil that cannot be averted otherwise; and (2) where tolerating an evil secures a greater benefit than not doing so, and there is no other way to secure this benefit. Good, on the other hand, may be forfeited under two conditions: (1) where its forfeiture is for the sake of a greater good; and (2) where its procurement entails evil whose harm is greater than the would-be benefit of the good in question. This applies to ('difficult cases' of) weighing quotidian good and evil according to the calculus of religion. As for set-

ting aside religious obligations where they result in undue worldly harm or allowing forbidden acts due to some worldly need—such as setting aside the obligation to fast while traveling, or allowing acts normally forbidden in a state of ritual preparedness for pilgrimage, or setting aside a pillar of prayer due to illness—all of this falls under the general latitude characterizing the religion as a whole and the principle of removing undue constraints, as we alluded to at the beginning of this discussion."

34 On this understanding, it is not possible for a command of the Lawgiver to contradict an authentic religious interest of the people or even an authentic worldly interest, as Imām al-Shāṭibī pointed out in his book *al-Muwāfaqāt*. Even if an act appears on its face to be consistent with the Lawgiver's will, that is, it is based on a legally grounded command or prohibition, but the interest it serves (via this or that application) is inconsistent with the Lawgiver's will, such an act must be deemed inappropriate and illegal. For the acts legislated by the religious law are not intended for their own sake; rather, something else is intended by them, namely, their presumed effects [under normal or ideal circumstances]. And these are the interests in consideration of which these acts were legislated. On this understanding, were there to exist a command or prohibition that represented a particular interest but whose application coincided with the forfeiture of a higher interest, it would be forbidden to act on the basis of that command or prohibition, as "Shaykh al-Islam" Ibn Taymīya pointed out in his *fatwā* collection:

35 "If interests and harms come into competition or conflict with each other, then even if a particular command or prohibition entails the procurement of an interest or the avoidance of a harm, one must examine the conflict: if the interest that will be forfeited

or the harm that will obtain (by implementing this command or prohibition) is greater, the act in question cannot be considered to be commanded (by the Lawgiver); rather, if the harm that will obtain is greater than the interest likely served, this act must be deemed forbidden."[15]

36 Now, this topic of conflicting interests and granting preference to one over the other is a broad one. As such, scholars have gone into great detail regarding this matter in ways that would not be appropriate to include in such an abbreviated treatise as this. It may be of benefit, however, to note that vital interests take precedence, in cases of conflict, over valued interests; and valued interests take precedence over supplementary interests. Similarly, basic interests take precedence over complementary ones. Nay, vital interests themselves even vary in degree of importance. Thus, the interest of preserving religion takes precedence over that of preserving life;[16] and the interest of preserving life takes precedence over that of preserving the integrity of the rational faculties, and so forth and so on. Also, where apparently equal interests and harms come into conflict, avoidance of harm is granted precedence over the procurement of benefit, as we alluded to in explaining the proofs with which we opened this topic.

37 The essence of what we have adduced regarding this topic may be summarized, thus, in the following precepts:

1. It is absolutely necessary to consider the likelihood of realizing or forfeiting scripturally recognized interests in any action undertaken by any Muslim individual or group.
2. Legally recognized implicit interests, including those based on absolute certainty as well as those based on reasonable certainty, are the universal vital interests.

3. Interests are ranked according to the importance attached to their consideration: vital, then valued, then supplementary.
4. The religious law gives preference to the highest interest and seeks to avoid the greatest harm.
5. If, considering the interest behind a command or prohibition, its implementation turns out to entail a greater harm or forfeit a greater interest, it becomes forbidden to implement this command or prohibition.
6. The avoidance of harm is given precedence over the procurement of benefit.[17]

38 These foundational principles are virtually a point of consensus among all legal theoreticians; and many proofs from the Qur'ān and Sunna converge to support them. Thus, it is incumbent upon scholars to bear them in mind when deriving legal rulings. And it is incumbent upon everyone who seeks to arrive at a *sharī'ah*-based decision to process his decision through these principles.

39 It remains now for us to apply these principles to the situation at hand, to clarify to us all that what has occurred is in violation of these agreed-upon, well-established, *sharī'ah*-based principles. This obliges us to stop and assess what is happening and then put it aright, in order to bring it into conformity with what we believe to be the aims of the Wise Lawgiver in this regard.

40 First we ask: Why has all of this occurred—this bloodshed, these wasted energies? Why have all these conflicts flared up and all these souls been put to waste between some of the Islamic movements and the government?

41 They will say: Have you not seen what has happened to us? Have the arbitrary incarcerations that afflict even the idle and lame not reached your ears? Have you not heard about the latest rounds

of incarcerations? Have you not heard about the barbaric torture that has left its mark on the bodies of hundreds of youth? Have you not heard about the mosques and homes that have been violated and of the furnishings that have been destroyed? Have you not heard about the womenfolk who have been humiliated and the children who have been terrorized? Has what has been said about "striking people in the depths of their hearts" not reached you?[18] And have you not heard about the interdictions imposed on missionary work and about religiously enthusiastic youth being prevented from calling people to God and mounting the pulpits? Do you not see that all of these things compel us to take up arms to defend our selves and our mission?

42 We return to ask: What is the aim or aims of taking up arms and putting all of these souls to waste?

43 They will say: To stop to these incarcerations and this torture, and to bring about humane treatment and the freedom to call people to God.

44 We return to ask: Is this the appropriate way to realize these aims? And after all this horrific experience, the bitterness of which you have tasted over these past years in which blood has flowed like rivers, souls have been put to waste, Muslims have fought each other—and some have died!—have these goals been realized? Have the incarcerations stopped; or have the prisons continued to be packed with prisoners, the situation going from a problem of dozens of prisoners—or, let us say, hundreds according to the worst estimates—to a problem of thousands being crowded into prisons and even having new prisons built to accommodate them? Has the violation of homes and mosques stopped; or has it increased and been redoubled, to the point that homes no longer enjoy any sanctity? Have you obtained the freedom to call people to God

and the right to mount the pulpit; or has your mission been smitten in its vital areas, to the point that your mission no longer has a place in the pulpit or anywhere else? Then, has the "striking people in the depths of their hearts" stopped; or has it increased and its scope widened to the point that it has become the rule (rather than the exception), either through bullets on the streets, torture in the prisons, or neglecting the sick to the point that they die in prison of their illnesses? Have you put an end to the killing; or has it increased many times over?

45 Now, we will not go on talking about what should be. Rather, we must stop and evaluate what has happened, in order to correct (what was incorrect about) it. And to this end we say the following:

46 First, any and all acts should be regulated according to *sharīʿah*-based interests. This applies whether we are talking about the initial execution of acts or redirecting them in the event that they should veer off course once undertaken. In other words, anyone who makes a decision to do a thing with the proviso that the benefit of doing so outweighs the harm, only to discover, either before he begins the action or after he enters into it, that the harm of doing so is preponderant or, even worse, that the presumed interest will not be served at all, should immediately desist from such an action.

47 Now, without doubt, after all of this long experience, it has been confirmed that all of this spilled blood and all these brutal battles have not served any legitimate interests to be mentioned. On the contrary, dozens of harms, all of which should have been avoided, have come as a consequence. The spilled blood and wasted souls of the sons of a single religion, not to mention the vendettas and mutual hatred that have filled their souls and the prisons that burst at the seams with youth; all of these things constitute a

great harm. Nay, they constitute numerous harms, which, without doubt, we should all stop and take a moment to put an end to and (try to) reverse their negative effects, especially since no interest was actually served by any of this. How could there be, when there was no viable legitimate interest present to begin with?

48 Thus, blood, effort, and money have all been spent to no avail, at a time when we need all of these in our battle against the real enemy at whose hands all of our Muslim peoples suffer and regarding the identity of which no one differs: poverty and underdevelopment! This is in addition to the external enemy who lies in wait for us, our religion, and our homeland.

49 Now, one may say: And what about all the injustice and oppression from which we suffer? To this we say: Be steadfast! And we believe that the reward of steadfastness in such circumstances is more hope-inspiring and weightier in the scales of deeds on the Day of Judgment.[19]

50 In sum, we must pool our efforts to end these activities from which nothing comes but destruction for the followers of a single religion. And maybe this will be an auspicious beginning upon which we can build a solution that mitigates all of this suffering and gives everyone the opportunity to contribute practically to addressing the concerns of this country and relieving its affliction.

51 These are the *sharīʿah*-based interests of us all as Muslims living on a single planet and in a single country. And securing the interests of this country requires the efforts of us all, to retrieve a sense of well-being, forward movement, and rebirth. And above all else, the interests of this religion oblige us to join efforts to raise its stature and call the people to it and to wipe away the stains of all of the despicable propaganda that has so disfigured its upright approach.

52 Yes, the interest of this religion, whose enemies have exploited this strife and the bloodshed that has raged among its followers to the end of tarnishing its image and portraying it as bloodthirsty and terroristic, to the point that the outside world has come to view the Muslim as a symbol of terrorism and bloodletting. In the face of all of this, it is in the interest of us all to stand firm against these harms, hoping for the reward of God and yearning for His grace and mercy.

Chapter Two: A Reality-Based Assessment

53 It is clear error to assume positions, establish rulings, or issue *fatwās* removed from a consideration of actual reality on the ground and a comprehensive assessment of its implications, considering this a fundamental pillar upon which *fatwās* must be based. Indeed, all rulings and all *fatwās* should recline upon two fundamental constituents: (1) reality on the ground and its implications; and (2) *sharīʿah* proofs, represented by the Qur'ān, Sunna, or other recognized sources of legislation.

54 And the truth is that any impartial observer of the reality of the conflict that has raged between some Islamic movements and the police will find that the Muslims of this country—be they from the Islamist movements or the police—are the most harmed by this conflict and the least to benefit from it. Indeed, every potential benefit to be derived from all this blood, all these energies, and all this money has poured into the coffers of the enemies of this religion and this country.

55 Numerous parties seek to exploit these events in order to promote their own specific interests, interests that routinely contradict the most vital concerns of the country. And in order to promote these advantages, they seek to keep these conflicts raging, by means of encouraging or inciting them or by assisting one or both sides, in order to increase the flames of conflict in intensity. And though their specific aims and positions may vary, they are all in agreement in not desiring any good for any of us. They agree on trying to keep the flames of civil strife ablaze in order to bring them closer to realizing their nefarious aims.

56 We will allude here to the most prominent of these parties, on both the international and domestic levels, as well as their aims in seeking to perpetuate this civil strife among us.

Israel

57 Without doubt, Israel is the first beneficiary. For Egypt is the real center of gravity in any confrontation with the Hebrew state, be it military, cultural, or civilizational. For this reason, anything that stands to weaken this country and keep it turned inward upon its domestic concerns, as its internal problems rage out of control, will find Jewish encouragement. These very sentiments have peppered the statements of their officials as well as the writings of their journalists and writers. For example, Yitzhak Rabin announced during his first visit to Europe and America that his first priority would be to combat the spread of "fundamentalism" in the region, this being a term they apply to Islamist movements. Then he called upon the international community to join him in solidarity in facing this threat!

58 Naturally, he will not seek to use his soldiers or his army to combat this spread. He will seek to do so, rather, by means of igniting strife among these movements and their governments, in order to stoke war between them. In this way, he will weaken both sides, and both sides will be diverted away from standing up against Zionist expansion by their preoccupation with each other. Indeed, Netanyahu made similar declarations during his first visit to America, maybe using the same or even more explicit words. In fact, you almost never hear an address or declaration by him that does not directly or indirectly convey this meaning. Thus, while the political party or the political platform may differ, the goal remains the same.

59 But the gravity of the situation increases further, as we hear the drums of war beat all around us and the entire region grows anxious and fearful of war, watching the Israeli prime minister trample upon every international law and convention, threatening everyone around him, as he wallows in his pipedream of an indomitable army and a greater Israel stretching from the Nile to the Euphrates! Without doubt, the danger here is compounded when we note Israel's role in the region as it seeks to implement its strategy of military and economic domination. This role continues to increase in prominence, while the role of the Arabs and Muslims shrinks, because most Islamic countries are turned in on themselves and their internal problems and concerns. This dreaded war undoubtedly threatens the region, while our energies are wasted or devoted to causes entirely removed from any concern with this anticipated conflict.

60 Beyond this, even if there is no actual war, another type of aggression, whose effect is no less dangerous than that of war, continues to pierce our borders, though there is less awareness of this

and virtually no precautions taken against it. Jews try to weaken Muslims in neighboring countries by spreading corruption and vice, destroying the economy and undermining self-confidence. They try to weaken morale and sow despair by spreading myths about Israel's alleged power and the impossibility of confronting it, and about its nuclear program and the stockpile of nuclear weapons it is supposed to be preparing for its coming war with the Arabs. This is not to mention (the dissemination of) drugs, involvement in espionage, and other such forms of aggression.

61 Both of these forms of war clearly require the joining of efforts and the pooling of resources to strengthen our domestic front in our confrontation with Israel, even as they require that we close ranks in the face of these various attempts to violate (our national integrity).

62 This attempt to marginalize or neutralize the role of Egypt, which will undoubtedly persist given the weakness that continues to spread through the body of our Islamic Community, is among the greatest dangers to the future of our struggle with the Jewish state. At the same time, forcing Egypt to succumb to these attempts to marginalize or neutralize her role, because of her preoccupation with internal struggles, will have the menacing effect of encouraging a policy of Israeli intransigence in the region and of forfeiting the rights of our Muslim peoples, both within and without Palestine. It will deny the Palestinian people support from the largest Arab country—and the largest power—in the region that could aid them in their legitimate struggle in which they have now come to stand alone with no supporter, facing an Israeli war machine that is backed by all the countries of the West. This war machine is now completely free to devote itself to the Palestinian issue, since all the Arabs and Muslims have been diverted away

from playing any meaningful role in aiding, supporting, or sending any help to the Palestinians. Israel is now free to deal with them alone, confident that the way is clear of anything that might be a cause for concern.

63 This is clearly a multifaceted war that will require that every available hand and every drop of blood be put to proper use and be brought to bear on an epic conflict that takes priority over all others.

America and the West

64 In his book, *Seize the Moment: America's Challenge in a One-Superpower World*,[20] former American President Richard Nixon specified that, following the collapse of the Soviet Union, the next enemy will be fundamentalist Islamic movements. The leaders of NATO conveyed similar sentiments following the collapse of communism, and set out to hold meetings with officials in the region on the pretext of supporting the latter in their confrontation with terrorism. The real aim, of course, was to provoke an escalation of this confrontation with Islamic movements, with plainly false promises to support and prop up these governments. The truth is that the West's attempt to foment against Islamic movements and fan the flames does not aim to promote the interests of Muslim countries or to bring them prosperity and stability. Rather, there are numerous other objectives, all of which serve something other than the interests of our people and our plundered rights. They refuse to recognize the leadership role of Egypt, the leader in the region by virtue of what her historical, civilizational, and demographic weight impose upon her. And they strive to shrink or neu-

tralize that role or to limit its effectiveness by way of distracting her with internal problems.

65 The secret behind these attempts is their desire to see Israel supplant Egypt's leadership role in the region, alongside their struggle to establish Israel's economic and political dominance over the region and its leaders. Clearly, however, the historical depth of Egypt's confrontations with Israel, its standing up to Israeli efforts at expansion, and its guarding the interests of the countries of the region vis-à-vis Israel, not to mention its military and civilizational weight in this confrontation—these are all considered fundamental dangers that threaten the Jewish expansion that America and the West supports. In this way, the interests of the West and America converge with the interests of the Jews in perpetuating these internal confrontations in order to take Egypt out of this battle and leave the field wide open for all of them to rampage about as they please.

66 The West's interests lie in propping up Israel as a Western military outpost and a bridge over which to extend Western hegemony over the region. In addition, their interests lie in seizing control over the riches of these countries, including oil and other raw materials, which, to their minds, are not the proper entitlement of peoples who devote themselves to fighting to secure their destiny, preserve their rights, and bring about material comfort and the proper investment of their energies. Rather, they [the West] are only contented with peoples who are preoccupied with internal conflicts that turn them away from the battle for development and advancement.

67 These are the interests of the West in the region—without doubt, in complete conflict with the interests of our peoples, who need to marshal every effort to free themselves of the need for

Western aid and to establish relations with the West on the basis of equality and mutual interests. Indeed, among the things that exacerbate this problem is the constant need for American aid, which the Americans use as a carrot to be dangled before our countries any time we take a position grounded in national solidarity in which we seek to protect our rights and the rights of the Palestinian people, in disregard of the interests of the West. This imposes upon us that we take a united stand that obliges us to work to keep our national will free and independent, placing the Egyptian prerogative beyond the hegemonic attempts and pressures directed at her decision-makers in order to get them to alter their course. All of this requires that we coordinate our efforts and unite in our struggle. Egypt's stature, which her civilizational weight imposes upon her, especially in the context of the new world order, which recognizes no place for the weak and knows nothing but the law of the jungle, obliges us all to struggle together to pool our efforts in order to place our country in her natural position of leadership and to force others to respect this stature.

The Secularists

68 Of course, we do not accuse all of them of flouting the interests of the nation in pursuit of personal or particular group interests. Indeed, there are many of them—in fact, one might say a majority—who understand that the interests of the country reside in coordinating our efforts to face the true enemy of the nation. And they extend their hands to everyone who strives in this path, even if they disagree with them in ideology or creed. And this, without doubt, is a position worthy of respect. In fact, we would

often read about this majority calling upon the government, even if in a low voice, to safeguard the Islamic trend, considering the latter a nationalist trend, and to benefit from its efforts to advance the wheel of development and raise the stature of the nation, instead of escalating its confrontation with this trend, which would only bring harm to both sides.

69 Obviously, our focus is not on these people but on a minority of secularists who disregard the interests of the country, along with the rights of brotherhood and neighborliness, who no longer look to anything but their own interests, even if the realization of these should come upon the ruins of our country and our people. As we said, they are a small minority. But they have a loud voice that has filled the earth with its rumpus, inciting society against the Islamist groups, calling for war against them and for their annihilation, using every manner of demagoguery that could be spewed to instigate and incite.

70 Without doubt, these people do not seek to promote the interests of the country. Rather, as they say, they see an opportunity therein for the "reactionary forces," that is, the government and the Islamist groups, as they claim, to fight against and thus weaken each other in order to enable *them* to take over power and banish those who remain in opposition to their program. Indeed, we may never forget the statement of a famous communist, who was an attorney in one of the cases involving the Islamist groups some years ago: "I hope to see the maximum number of death sentences handed down in this case, resulting in acts of retribution between the Islamist groups and the government, igniting a struggle for vengeance and utterly exasperating both sides."

71 The truth is that the influence this little special-interest mafia has come to exercise over parts of the media has been a serious fac-

tor in inciting efforts to ignite the fires of confrontation and bury alive every attempt to quell these incidents and bring them to an end. Everyone will probably remember how they were a factor in bringing down a former minister of the interior who strove to bring success to an intercession effort by a leading group of clergy that sought to stem the torrent of blood and put an end to this long dispute. Everyone will probably remember how the newspapers jumped all over him and accused him of dereliction, weakness, and compromising the dignity of the state, as they claimed. And in their attack on him, they breached all the ethics and standards of journalism, all of which had an effect on precipitating the end of his days in the ministry.[21]

72 Without a doubt, these people constitute a stumbling block in the path of every effort to end these circumstances, even as their efforts threaten to reduce this country, including its aspirations and its needs, to a lifeless corpse. They consider the continuation of this confrontation to be a realization of their goal of trying to widen the scope of their influence and gain control over the resources of the country. Shall we, then, not deny them this opportunity, by standing shoulder to shoulder and cooperating with each other to bring about unity and assistance to the True Faith?

Chapter Three: Correcting Misunderstandings

73 There can be no doubt that the confrontations that have raged between various factions of young men and the police apparatus have generated numerous, important, and serious issues that re-

quire constant recalibration on the basis of *sharī'ah*. At the same time, there can be no doubt that the turbulence of war, the clanking of swords, and the mutual outcries for vengeance and retribution have prevented the people of authentic *sharī'ah* knowledge from voicing their opinion on these important matters. The inevitable result, whether we like it or not, is that certain understandings, which took shape under the influence of the violent pressure tactics that were routinely applied and the unnatural circumstances that generally prevailed, will settle in the minds of these young men. And many of these understandings will be unsound and inconsistent with the religious law, whether we are talking about the latter's detailed, specific rulings or its overall spirit and general principles.

74 We are all aware of what is occurring in one of our neighboring countries after five years of violent confrontations, during which large segments of Muslim youth ended up embracing the ideology of excommunication (*takfīr*) as a violent, untempered reaction to the maniacal tactics of the police and popular defense militias.

75 Now, we do not deny that here in Egypt an element of extremism has befallen some factions' understanding of the concept of jihad, to the point that this understanding needs to be recalibrated on the basis of *sharī'ah*. And we fear that if matters persist as they are and the flames of vengeance continue to smolder in peoples' hearts that the matter will get out of hand, the tear in the fabric will expand beyond any mender's ability, and it will no longer fall within the capacity of anyone to return matters to their proper course. Similarly, we fear that the continuation of these confrontations will generate new misunderstandings that become normalized with the passing of time, to the point that those who hold such understandings, due to their long familiarity with them,

come to believe that they are factually consistent with *sharī'ah* and that there is nothing wrong with them. In fact, subsequent generations will come to receive these notions as if they were the very core and spirit of religion. We all remember, for example, that the period of persecution in the prisons of the 1960s produced an ideology of excommunication, the effects of which still persist among many of those groups that are given to unsanctioned innovation.
76 As a warning against the likes of this, out of a yearning to avoid its repetition, and due to our desire to avert the effects of some of the things that have already happened, we deemed it necessary to write something in which we clarify what we deem to be correct regarding these matters. And we have tried to restrict ourselves to the most important misunderstandings whose first indications have already appeared or whose emergence and normalization we fear might be looming. We have found that the most important of these could be classified under four basic categories:

1. That which pertains to understandings of jihad that are wrong, imprecise, extremist in nature, or confused. And in order to correct these understandings we set out to write this epistle. It is our plan, however, God* willing, to write something more comprehensive regarding the legal impediments to fighting, according to *sharī'ah.*
2. That which pertains to religious extremism, the abandonment of religious moderation, and the tendency to transgress bounds in response to the actions of some who violate religion and its edicts by flouting and giving them short shrift.
3. That which pertains to the theology of excommunication, such as excommunicating those who commit major

sins, or refusing to recognize ignorance as an excuse on (detailed) matters of theology, or extending a verdict of excommunication over entire groups, based on their purported federation with others upon whom a verdict of excommunication has been levied.

4. That which pertains to the People of the Book and transgressing the bounds in dealing with them and discounting the value of their lives and property, with no consideration for the value of justice as an elevated Islamic commitment.

77 Inasmuch as the present installment is limited, as we have mentioned, to a treatment of some of the misunderstandings surrounding the matter of jihad, it is our hope that God* will facilitate the way to our issuing a series of writings dedicated to correcting other misunderstandings that have already settled in people's minds or that we fear may soon emerge.

78 Of course, many of our overzealous brethren will rise in protest, saying: "You assail our ears and chide your brothers for some of their violations that have occurred, or you warn them about anticipated violations. But how can these be compared with the security apparatus's violations—which everyone, near and far, knows well—of Muslim youth and Muslim society, nay, of the very call to God and of the homeland? Why do you not talk of issuing broad proclamations, lengthy treatises, and numerous pages about these things? Has it not been said: 'If a litigant comes before you with his eye plucked out, do not pass judgment until you see his adversary; for the latter may have both eyes plucked out?'"[22]

79 We respond, first: God forbid that our counsel to our brethren and our beloved in the Faith, who occupy a place in the profoundest depths of our hearts, should be intended as an assault or

a chiding. On the contrary, this is an attempt to engage in a mutual enjoining of truth and to direct people toward that which is good, as our Lord* and our Prophet• have commanded us.

80 Second, we say: It is not lost on us that throughout these confrontations the other side has committed many violations—nay, very many violations!—that deserve criticism.

81 Third, we say: We simply address those who will receive our counsel and listen with open ears to our directives. As for the other side, the security apparatus, they naturally look upon themselves as being above and beyond anything we have to say, one way or the other. And this is clear to all.

82 Fourth, we say: We are duty-bound to examine our actions, perceptions, and understandings in light of the religious law, regardless of our opinion about the extent to which others conform to or violate the latter.

The Legal Impediment

83 Legal theorists define the legal impediment as "that the existence of which preempts the existence of something else." In other words, it is a thing whose existence preempts the implementation of a legal rule, such as fatherhood in the case of the retaliatory options governing intentional, aggressive homicide. Al-Shawkānī (d. 1255/1839) states in his book on legal theory, *Irshād al-fuḥūl ilā taḥqīq al-ḥaqq min 'ilm al-uṣūl:* "A legal impediment is a concrete, palpable phenomenon whose existence entails an underlying consideration that in turn entails the nonimplementation of a legal rule or the nonefficiency of a legal cause."[23] Prior to this, al-Āmidī (d. 631/1233) had put forth a similar statement. And Dr. 'Abd al-

Wahhāb Khallāf (d. 1375/1956) states in his definition: "The legal impediment is that the existence of that which entails the nonimplementation of a rule or the nullification of a legal cause." Legal theorists divide it into two types, according to whether it affects a legal rule itself or the actual legal cause underlying a legal rule.

84 An example of a legal impediment that affects the implementation of a legal rule itself would be an heir's murder of someone he lawfully inherits from. This affects the rule on inheritance and blocks the transfer of wealth. An example of a legal impediment that affects a legal cause underlying a legal ruling would be the presence of debt on the part of one who holds wealth equal to the threshold amount requiring the payment of obligatory alms (*zakāt*). This impediment affects the actual legal cause that gives rise to the obligation to pay alms, which is holding wealth equal to the threshold amount, as is well known. Thus, one who holds wealth equal to the threshold amount is not obligated to pay alms, even if a full fiscal year should pass on his holdings, if he has a debt whose payment would bring his wealth below the threshold amount or consume it entirely. Debt in this case is called a legal impediment. And this impediment affects the implementation of the legal rule, despite the full presence of the legal cause, which is holding wealth equal to the threshold amount.

85 It is likewise in the case of jihad. There are legal causes that make it obligatory, such as the presence of hostile aggression, or a danger that threatens the lands or people of Islam, or civil strife and the like, all of which give rise to the obligation to wage jihad, either defensively or preemptively. Similarly, there are legal impediments whose occurrence, jointly or in isolation, preempt the implementation of the rule obligating jihad and come between Muslims and this obligation.

86 These are the legal impediments about which we shall speak presently in some detail. But, before we cite them and back them with proof from the Qur'ān and Sunna and clarify their contours through the views of the Community's scholars and Pious Ancestors, we would like to clarify that some of the expressions and phrases used by the Pious Ancestors in their *fatwā*s may not be fully applicable to the reality we live today. Today, our discourse is focused on the fighting between a group of young Muslim men and police officers and officials. And as is well known, we do not consider the latter to be Unbelievers. Yet, the expressions handed down from the scholars of the past deal with fighting between Muslims and Unbelievers. It is thus necessary to draw attention to this difference, lest some should think that by relying on these statements we aim to excommunicate individual members of the police force, even though this is not our position.
87 If it is asked, "Why, then, do you adduce these statements?" We respond, "We adduce them for two reasons: first, as proof that the legal impediments we shall mention are valid impediments that have been endorsed by jurists among the Ancestors; second, to substantiate the argument that if a legal impediment was considered valid in their time and in consideration of prototypical Unbelievers whose Unbelief is a matter of unanimous consensus, then it should be considered all the more valid today in considering fighting between two groups—the Muslim youth and the police—neither of which judges the other to be Unbelievers."
88 It remains for us to mention that we will be citing these legal impediments in summary fashion—those that are specific to our circumstances as well as those that are more general in scope—on an equal footing and on the understanding that there are much

broader details attaching to each of these impediments. Perhaps God* will facilitate the way for us to clarify these soon.

Legal Impediments to Fighting

Impediment One

If It Predominates in One's Thinking That Jihad Will Not Realize the Interest for Which It Was Legislated

89 It is known that jihad has not been legislated for its own sake and is not pursued for what it entails in the way of letting blood, annihilating spirits, killing people, and amputating limbs. Rather, it has been legislated for the purpose of realizing a rightful interest —or interests—in the way of aiding religion and putting down civil and geopolitical strife and other such causes.

90 Ibn 'Ābidīn° (d. 1258/1842) stated in this regard: "Jihad is only for the purpose of fortifying faith and establishing canonical prayer. Its goodness lies thus in what it promotes other than itself." He also said, regarding the intended goal of jihad, "It is the emptying of the earth of corruption." Ibn Daqīq al-'Īd (d. 702/1302) said, "The default position is not to destroy souls. This has simply been allowed to the extent dictated by the need to repel harm." And "Shaykh al-Islam," Aḥmad b. 'Abd al-Ḥalīm Ibn Taymīya (d. 728/1328) made a similar declaration, adding: "Killing people, including Unbelievers, is a harm. It has simply been allowed in view of a (greater) interest.

91 Thus, if it predominates in one's thinking that jihad will not bring about the interest for which it was legislated, its legality is

thereby nullified and it ceases to be a desideratum of the religious law. That is to say, the law and its machinery cease to address legally responsible persons with this obligation. And whoever embarks upon jihad, despite this knowledge that its aim will not be realized, is not among those about whom the Messenger of God• said, "Whoever fights to render God's word highest proceeds in the path of God."[24] On the contrary, he comes close to being included among those about whom the Messenger of God• spoke when he was asked about who actually proceeds in the path of God: a man who fights for booty; a man who fights to be remembered; and a man who fights in order for people to observe his stature? He responded, "Whoever fights to render God's word highest proceeds in the path of God."[25] Thus, if it predominates in one's thinking that fighting will not elevate the word of God and His law, it ceases to be permissible for one to plunge into it. And whoever does so simply fights out of bravado, or fanaticism, or in order for people to observe his stature, or some similar purpose. And all of these motives are condemned.

92 Al-Shāṭibī° said, in one of his precious statements: "Since it has been established that legal rules are legislated to serve human interests, actions are assessed on the basis thereof; for these interests are the actual goal of the Lawgiver." Thus, if an action is outwardly and inwardly consistent with the aim for which it was legislated, there is no problem. But if it is outwardly consistent while the intended interest is violated, this act is neither sound nor legitimate. For legally sanctioned acts are not intended for themselves but simply for other considerations, namely, their entailments, which are the actual interests for which they were legislated.

93 It remains to be mentioned that if neither party to an armed conflict, in this case the young men of the Islamic movements and

the police, charges the other with Unbelief or of falling outside the pale of the Faith, and this fighting does not lead to the realization of any legitimate interest, we should rush to put an end to it. For the spilled blood is Muslim blood, even if some of those involved are guilty of injustices or aggression against the others or each party at least accuses the other of this.

Impediment Two

If Fighting Conflicts with Guiding Humanity

94 It is known that the wisdom behind sending messengers and revealing scriptures is to guide the people. Thus, God* said to his His Messenger•: *O Prophet, We have sent you as a witness, a bearer of good tidings and as a warner, a caller to God by His permission and a radiant lamp* [33:45–46]. And He said: *Verily We have sent you as a witness, a bearer of good tidings and a warner* [48:8]. And He said: *But We rendered it a light by which We guide whomever We please from among Our servants. And verily you guide to a straight path, the path of God to Whom belongs what is in the heavens and what is in the earth. Do not all affairs ultimately terminate with God?* [42:52–53]. Now, the Muslim Community has inherited this mission from its Prophet, the mission of guiding humanity. God* said: *Let there be among you a community who beckons to good, commands what is right and forbids what is evil. They shall be the successful ones* [3:104].

95 Our Messenger• has encouraged us to invite people to God and to strive to guide them. He said, "That God should guide through you a single man is better for you than your coming to own the most exceptionally high-bred camels."[26] He also said, "Whoever calls to guidance earns a reward equal to that of those

who answer his call, without this diminishing anything from the reward of the latter."[27]

96 And his caliphs who came immediately after him•, used to say: "Verily, God* sent Muḥammad• as a guide; He did not send him as a revenue collector." And the Qur'ānic verses and Prophetic reports in this regard, including those with full, incomplete, and broken chains, are many and well known. Thus, guiding the people is the apex priority of any Islamic movement that purports to follow in the footsteps of the Messenger•. For through this, servitude to God* is realized. Fighting, for its part, was only legislated to serve the call to God and protect it from outside aggression, to open the path before it and crush the forces of pre-Islamic ignorance that would prevent this call from making its way to all people. Fighting was never intended for itself, as an end.

97 There are hadith—some of which have already been mentioned—in which the Prophet• commanded the generals of his army to place ahead of any campaign a call to the enemy to come to God. And the jurists are in agreement on the impermissibility of fighting anyone whom the call has not reached before inviting him to God. They even say that if the call has already reached them, it is recommended that it be repeated. Similarly, they agree that anyone who seeks asylum in order to hear the Qur'ān and to know exactly what this religion entails must be granted asylum. And it becomes forbidden to kill or fight him, so that he may hear the Word of God. After that, we are obligated to deliver him to safe quarters, whether he accepts or rejects the truth.[28]

98 Similarly, they are in unanimous agreement on recognizing the right of People of the Book to remain in Muslim lands on the basis of a treaty of protection (*'aqd al-dhimmah*). The wisdom behind this is to make it easy for them to hear the words of guidance

and be influenced by the religion, such that they might embrace Islam. Indeed, this is what actually happened in many lands following the Islamic conquests. In fact, the overwhelming majority of prophets were not commanded to engage in armed struggle, nor did they engage their peoples in battle. They were simply commanded to deliver the message, call the people to God, establish proofs for what they were calling to, and debate with their peoples in the most seemly manner.

99 In a similar fashion, our Prophet• went on for over a decade in Mecca simply calling the people to God, not having permission to fight, not even defensively or in order to repel aggression. When he was finally given permission to fight, the mission of calling people to God remained in operation side by side with jihad.[29] All of this points to the fact that guiding the people is the highest priority and that calling people to God and delivering and clarifying the message take precedence over armed conflict and lining up for battle.

100 Ibn Isḥāq (d. 152/769) narrated, through a chain he adduced going all the way back to the Prophet•, "Indeed for a single man to embrace Islam is more beloved to me than killing a thousand Unbelievers."[30] Thus, if calling people to God and jihad converge in a situation where both will independently lead to guiding humanity, clearly, calling people to God is to be given precedence and must be deemed sufficient. And what we have mentioned thus far provides ample proof of this. As for instances where jihad does not lead to the desired outcome but has the opposite effect or serves no interest at all, and simply calling people to God comes to constitute the effective remedy, calling people to God becomes the lone duty and the only obligation with which no other obligation can compete.

101 Thus, "Shaykh al-Islam" Ibn Taymīya° said: "If two obligations compete with each other and cannot be mutually accommodated such that precedence is given to the more pressing of them, the other ceases to be an obligation. And one who abandons the lesser for the more pressing of these has not really abandoned any obligation." This is a really valuable statement. So ponder it!

Impediment Three

Incapacity, Specifically, Lack of Physical Capability

102 God* said, *God places on no soul an obligation greater than its capacity* [2:286]. And He* said, *Be mindful of your duty to God to the extent that you are able* [64:16]. And He* said, *God places on no soul an obligation greater than the capabilities He has granted it* [65:7]. And He said, *God has not levied upon you anything in the religion that would be a cause of distress* [22:78]. All of the scholars, to a person, have unanimously agreed, from the beginning of Islam down to our present day, that the obligation to fulfill religious duties is contingent upon physical capability and that one who is incapacitated has no religious responsibility to begin with, that is, in effect, the Lawgiver has not addressed to him the commands or prohibitions that he has no capacity to fulfill.

103 Said "Shaykh al-Islām" Ibn Taymīyah°: "Physical capability, ability, capacity, and potential are all implied stipulations in every affair. God* said, *Be mindful of your duty to God to the extent that you are able* [64:16]. And He* said, *God places on no soul an obligation greater than its capacity* [2:286]. And He said, *God places on no soul an obligation greater than the capabilities He has granted it* [65:7]. *Pilgrimage to the Sacred House is a duty to God upon all who are able*

to find their way thereto [3:97]. *No shame is there on the weak, the sick, or those who are unable to find financial means, as long as they are sincere to God and His Messenger* [9:91]."

104 Al-Shāṭibī° said: "The physical capability to carry out an action is a legal prerequisite or a legal cause underlying every commanded act. Thus, it is not admissible, according to the religious law, to hold a legally responsible person responsible for anything he is incapable of performing." Ibn 'Ābidīn stated in his famous supercommentary, *Radd al-Muḥtār*: "It is incumbent upon the Muslim ruler to dispatch a battalion to enemy lands once or twice each year, if it preponderates in his thinking that he has the means to stand up to them. Otherwise, it is not permissible for him to fight them." Shaykh Muḥammad b. 'Alā' al-Dīn al-Ḥaṣkafī (d. 1088/1677) stated verbatim in his commentary on *Tanwīr al-Abṣār*, also known as *al-Durr al-Mukhtār*: "{And it is necessary} due to its incumbent status {to consider} another stipulation, namely {ability}." And the author of *Tanwīr al-Abṣār* itself stated: "Its status as obligatory is contingent upon the physical capability to wield weapons." Ibn 'Ābidīn added in his supercommentary, "As well as the physical capability to fight, procure supplies and secure transportation"; up until he stated, "otherwise the obligation falls, because the degree of obedience required is commensurate with the amount of potential possessed. So ponder this."

105 If it is said, "What you and the scholars mention here regarding incapacity, lack of physical capability, or parity in weaponry with the enemy and the like, this is appropriate as proof against the obligation to wage jihad, not as a legal impediment to the duty to fulfill this obligation. And there is a big difference between the two. For incapacity preempts the obligation to perform an act; but it does not render the act impermissible. Thus, it seems that you

may have committed an oversight here in rendering these things legal impediments that actually render impermissible the act in question."

106 We respond: There is no oversight in rendering these things legal impediments. For jihad is among the gravest of issues, in that it entails rendering blood and property, nay even sexual intercourse, licit. And severe casualties routinely take place on both sides. Thus, if despite their incapacity and lack of ability, some people embark upon it, this will result in great harm, severe tribulation, and perdition for Muslims. From this perspective, there is nothing strange in our rendering incapacity and the like a legal impediment, not simply in and of itself but based on what it entails.

107 Dr. Muḥammad Sa'īd Ramaḍān al-Būṭī (d. 1434/2013) stated in his valuable work, *Fiqh al-Sīrah:* "The majority of jurists are in unanimous agreement that whenever Muslims are few in number or of insufficient preparedness such that it preponderates in their thinking that they will be killed should they decide to fight, while inflicting no casualties upon their enemy, the interest of preserving Muslim life is to be given precedence. For the realization of the competing interest, namely, preserving religion, is in this instance imaginary or almost certain not to obtain. And al-'Izz Ibn 'Abd al-Salām (d. 660/1261) confirms the impermissibility of delving into such a jihad, stating, 'If casualties are not inflicted upon the enemy, defeat of the Muslims must be the result. For in holding their position their souls will be forfeited, while the Unbelievers' breasts are soothed and the People of Islam are humiliated. Thus, holding their position here becomes a pure harm that entails no interest whatever.'"

108 I say—the speaker here being Dr. al-Būṭī: "Giving precedence to the interest of preserving life here is only apparent. As for

the reality of the situation, the interest served is that of religion, since under circumstances such as these the interest of religion dictates that the souls of the Believers remain intact, that they may go forth and wage jihad in other theaters of conquest. Otherwise, their destruction must be considered injurious to religion itself. In sum, it is incumbent to seek peace or to conceal the call to God whenever going public or engaging in armed conflict will bring harm to it." And the matter is as he stated.

Impediment Four

Self-Destruction

109 God* said, *And do not cast forth your hands into self-destruction* [2:195]. This is a countermand. And, according to what has been established in the science of legal theory, countermands entail prohibition. Thus, if jihad stands to realize nothing but the destruction, annihilation, and uprooting of the party that calls people to God and the wiping out of their call, there is no escaping the conclusion that it is thereby proscribed and prohibited.

110 Al-Shawkānī writes in his exegesis of this verse: "The truth is that what is considered in deducing meaning from Scripture are the general, lexical indications of expressions, not the specific concretions of their referents dictated by a particular historical context.[31] Thus, anything that can be said to be 'self-destruction' in matters of religion or worldly affairs is included in this meaning." Ibn Jarīr al-Ṭabarī (d. 310/923) concluded the same thing.

111 Among the things that would come under the dictates of this verse would be a man's rushing forth into battle and charging the enemy with no means of extracting himself nor of bringing about

any effect that would benefit the Muslim army. Ibn Abī Ḥātim reported on the authority of ʿAbd al-Raḥmān b. al-Aswad b. ʿAbd Yaghūth that they laid siege to Damascus and a man rushed toward the ranks of the enemy all by himself. The Muslims chided him for this and referred his matter to ʿAmr b. al-ʿĀṣ. The latter sent for him and then returned him, saying, "God* said, *And do not cast your hands forth into self-destruction.*"

112 If it is said, "But there are jurists who deem it permissible for an individual to plunge himself into the ranks of the enemy in pursuit of martyrdom," we respond: "They simply permitted this where there is an interest to be served thereby and where it aids to victory. As for instances where his plunging will simply lead to his death, accompanied by an increase in the audacity of the enemy and a sapping of the strength of the Muslims, there is no way to permit this. And were we to imagine that someone would permit it, this would only apply to an individual member of the army. As for the entire group that is dedicated to the cause of God and calling to His religion plunging itself into enemy ranks only to be killed with no hope of realizing victory or elevating the word of religion, it is unimaginable that this would be permitted under any circumstances."

113 Al-Shirāzī (d. 476/1083) stated, verbatim, in his famous book, *al-Muhadhdhab,* regarding the question of when an enemy numbers more than twice the Muslim army: "If it preponderates in their thinking that they will simply perish, there are two views: (1) that it is obligatory upon them to retreat, in accordance with His* statement, *And do not cast your hands forth into self-destruction;* (2) that it is recommended that they retreat, though not obligatory."

114 Thus, the least that he said regarding the Muslim army in such circumstances is that their fighting is discouraged. As for the

first view, it forbids fighting. And the view that states that it is forbidden should be recognized as the going opinion, especially where destruction will not be limited to the Muslim army but will spill over into the segment of the community that stands for truth, calls to guidance, and carries the flag of the Faith. And given that fighting will lead to this group's annihilation, the very least that can be said is that it is proscribed.

115 This contrasts the situation of our predecessors, when the army alone was exposed to destruction. As for the community of believers, the lands of Islam remained teeming with them. Also, it was easy for the Muslim ruler to replace a particular army. As for situations where the people of righteousness and guidance shrink in numbers and become limited to a few factions and small groups, it is not permissible to expose them to risk or to cast them into destruction. If it is said, "This is contradicted by the fact that martyrdom is recognized as praiseworthy. Indeed, how can you render it prohibited in some forms, when the Companions of the Prophet• pledged to defend their prophet to the death?"[32]

116 We respond, "There is no contradiction here. Al-Nawawī° (d. 676/1277) says: 'The meaning of pledging to defend to the death was that they would persevere even if doing so led to their death, not that death was the goal in and of itself.' Thus, seeking martyrdom is praiseworthy whenever advancing and persevering in jihad and exposing oneself to the causes of death through war and military maneuvers serve the interests of Islam. As for seeking martyrdom in the sense of aspiring to death and seeking it for its own sake, this has no basis, as was confirmed by al-Qurṭubī°. Now, this applies in the case of individuals or groups of individuals. How much more must it apply to entire communities and segments thereof? Without doubt, it is even more prohibited in their case."

117 And it may be that the likely destruction of the Muslims was one of the reasons behind the disallowance of jihad and its prohibition in Mecca, where the Muslims were a limited number of individuals in a pre-Islamic, pagan society, with no power and no defenses to protect them and no place in which they could seek asylum. But when the Messenger of God• and his Companions migrated to Medina and it became an Abode of Islam, jihad became permissible and then incumbent, since there was no longer any likelihood that the believing party would be annihilated. Yes, its army might be routed on occasion, as occurred at Uḥud. But for the entire community to be annihilated, this became highly unlikely. In fact, it may be impossible for any state to wipe any other state entirely out of existence. Indeed, this has never occurred, even in our own times, despite the use of the most devastating weapons. As for individual parties strewn throughout various lands and countries, it is easy to annihilate and eliminate them.

Impediment Five

The Presence of Muslims among a Non-Muslim Populace

118 According to one group of scholars, this is a legal impediment to fighting them, based on His* statement, *And were it not that you might trample upon believing men and believing women of whose presence you were unaware, by which action you would bring shame upon yourselves unwittingly [God would have permitted you to press your cause] that God might bring into His mercy whomever He pleases. Had they distinguished themselves from the others, We would have chastised the Unbelievers among them with a grievous chastisement* [48:25]. This was revealed in the matter of those powerless

Believers who were still in Mecca at the time of the Treaty of al-Ḥudaybīyah.[33] God did not permit His Messenger• to fight, in order to avoid harm coming to these people.

119 Al-Qurṭubī said in his exegesis of this verse: His* statement {and were it not for believing men . . . }, that is, powerless Believers in Mecca in the midst of the Unbelievers, such as Maslamah b. Hishām, 'Ayyāsh b. Abī Rabī'ah, Abū Jandal b. Suhayl, and their like; {of whose presence you were unaware}, that is, you did not know them; and it has been said that the meaning here is that you did not know that they were Believers; {that you might trample upon [them]}, by killing and assaulting them. And the cumulative meaning here is: Were it not that you might trample upon believing men and believing women of whose presence you were unaware, God would have permitted you to enter Mecca, and He would have granted you power over the Unbelievers. But We protected those who had remained there and hid their belief out of fear.

120 This verse is proof that the sanctity of Believers extends to the point of preserving Unbelievers, where it is not possible to harm Unbelievers without harming Believers. Abū Zayd said:[34] "I said to Ibn al-Qāsim, 'What do you think about a situation where the people of Islam lay siege to a group of polytheists holed up in one of their fortresses with Muslim captives; should this fortress be burned to the ground or not?' He replied, 'I heard Mālik (d. 179/795) being asked about whether a group of polytheists in their boats should be fired upon while they hold [Muslim] captives.' He said, 'Mālik responded, "I do not think they should, based on His* statement regarding the Meccans, *Had they distinguished themselves from the others, We would have chastised the Unbelievers among them with a grievous chastisement.*" Likewise, if an Unbe-

liever uses a Muslim as a human shield, it is not permissible to fire upon him. And if one does and causes the death of a Muslim, one must pay the weregild and expiate by manumission or fasting. If, however, they did not know of the Muslim's presence they are liable neither for the weregild nor expiation.'"

121 Ibn al-'Arabī (d. 543/1148) said in his book *Aḥkām al-Qur'ān*: "Mālik said, 'We had laid siege to the Byzantine city and cut off their water supply, such that they would send prisoners down to draw water for them and no one would be able to fire arrows upon them. Thus, they would be able to get water against our wishes.' Al-Shāfi'ī agreed with our (Mālikī) opinion. And the validity of this position is clear, as acquiring what is licit through illicit means is not permissible, especially where the price is a Muslim life. Thus, there is no appropriate position other than that of Mālik."

122 The hadith expert Ibn Kathīr° said: "{*And were it not for believing men and believing women*}, in their midst, who had concealed and hid their faith from their countrymen out of fear for their lives, We would have granted you power over them, such that you would kill and totally decimate them. But mixed in with them were pockets of believing men and women the existence of whom you would not have known at the time of attack. Thus, God* said {*that you might trample upon believing men and believing women of whose presence you were unaware, by which action you would bring shame upon yourselves*}, that is, sin and damages {*unwittingly*}, {*that God might bring into His mercy whomever He pleases*} or postpone their punishment in order to extract the Believers from among them, and so that many of them might return to Islam. Then He* said, {*Had they distinguished themselves from the others*}, that is, had the Unbelievers distinguished themselves from Believers in their midst {*We would have chastised the Unbelievers among them with a grievous*

chastisement}, that is, We would have granted you power over them such that you would inflict crushing casualties upon them."

123 It is stated in *al-Mudawwanah al-Kubrā*: "Ṣaḥnūn (d. 240/855) said, on the authority of al-Walīd, on the authority of someone who heard al-Awzaʿī (d. 157/774) say, regarding a group of Muslims who intercept an enemy ship containing Muslim captives, 'They should desist from burning this ship as long as there remains a single Muslim captive on it. In fact, a group of scholars have concluded that it is prohibited to fire upon Unbelievers if they take their own women and children as shields.'"

124 Al-Shawkānī said: "The hadiths addressing this matter indicate that it is not permissible to kill women and children. This is the conclusion of Mālik and al-Awzaʿī. For them, this is not permissible under any circumstance. Even if a non-Muslim enemy should take non-Muslim women and children as shields or seek refuge in a fortress or a ship, taking with them women and children, it would not be permissible to fire upon them nor to burn them out."

Impediment Six

A Nonbeliever's Declaring the Testimony of Faith, the Repentance of the Apostate, and His Returning to Islam, and the Return of the Rebel to Accepting Legitimate Authority

125 On the authority of ʿUmar b. al-Khaṭṭāb°: The Prophet• said, "I have been commanded to fight the people until they declare that there is no god but God. Thus, whoever declares that there is no god but God has rendered his property and his person safe from me, except by lawful right, and his ultimate reckoning rests with God."[35] On the authority of ʿUbayd Allāh b. ʿAdī on the au-

thority of Miqdād b. al-Aswad that the latter informed him that he once said, "O Messenger of God, what if I were to encounter a man from the Unbelievers who fought me and struck me with his sword cutting off one of my hands and then fled from me and sought refuge behind a tree, saying, 'I submit to God!'; should I go on to kill him, O Messenger of God, after he says this? The Messenger of God• said, 'Do not kill him.' I replied, 'O Messenger of God, he cut off my hand, then he said what he said after he had cut it off. Shall I kill him, O Messenger of God?' The Messenger of God• said, 'Do not kill him. If you kill him, he will acquire your status before you killed him, and you will acquire his status before he said the words he said.'"[36]

126 Usāmah b. Zayd° said: "The Messenger of God• sent us out on a campaign in which we showed up at the strongholds of the tribe of Juhaynah in the early morning. I caught up with one of their fleeing men, who exclaimed, 'There is no god but God.' I stabbed him with my sword anyway. Then I began to nurse doubts about my action, so I mentioned it to the Prophet•. The Messenger of God• replied, 'You killed him, despite his saying, "There is no god but God"?' I said, 'But he only said it out of fear of my weapon.' He responded, 'Did you not split open his heart so that you could see whether he actually said it from there or not?'"[37]

127 Abū Isḥāq al-Shirāzī (d. 476/1083) said: "Whenever an apostate repents, his repentance is accepted, be his apostasy publicly demonstrated or privately concealed, for example, in the form of denuding God of His attributes or embracing some form of crypto-infidelity. This is based on what was related on the authority of Anas°, who said, 'The Messenger of God• said, "I have been commanded to fight the people until they say, 'There is no god but God, Muhammad is the Messenger of God.' Whenever they tes-

tify that there is no god but God, face our direction of prayer, pray as we pray, and eat our slaughtered meat, their blood and money become unlawful to us except by a legally established right.'"[38] And if someone apostatizes, then reenters the faith, then apostatizes, then reenters the faith, and repeats this time and again, his act of reentering the faith is accepted, while he receives discretionary punishment for the carelessness he demonstrates toward religion.

128 Abū Isḥāq had commented: "His reentering the faith is not accepted if he repeats this time and again." But this is a mistake, as indicated by His* statement {*Say to the Unbelievers, "If you desist you will be forgiven for your previous misdeeds"*} [8:38]. This is also the case because he pronounced the twin testimony of faith after having apostatized. Thus, the status of his apostasy is as if he had apostatized once then reentered the faith. Shaykh al-Muṭīʿī (d. 1354/1935) said in his commentary on the *al-Muhadhdhab* of al-Shirāzī during his discussion of rebels: "If they return to recognizing legitimate authority, they are not to be fought (in accordance with God's statement): {*until they return to the command of God*}" [49:9].

Impediment Seven

If the Harms and Tribulations Attending Armed Conflict Are Greater Than the Anticipated Interests or If the Interests Forfeited Are Greater Than Those to Be Secured

129 This is clear and obvious. We have already mentioned a number of details in this regard in the first chapter. There we clarified that the harms and tribulations spawned by the fighting taking place today are far greater than any interest likely to obtain as a result thereof, as we also clarified that the interests that are forfeited are greater than those secured.

Impediment Eight

Pertaining Specifically to the People of the Book

130 The gist of this matter is that, if they pay (the tax on religious minorities (*jizyah*) to the ruler and he grants them a contract of protection, it becomes unlawful to fight them, whether they pay this in the name of the tax on religious minorities or by any other designation. As long as they express their desire to enter into a contract of protection with the Muslims, they must be granted this, and it becomes unlawful to bear arms against them.

131 On the authority of Buraydah°: "Whenever the Messenger of God• appointed a general over an army or battalion, he would exhort him to be mindful of God* regarding his personal conduct and to do good by the Muslims under his charge. Then he would say, 'Campaign in the name of God and in the path of God. Fight those who reject God, and execute your campaign without misappropriation, treachery, or bodily mutilation and without killing children. When you meet the enemy among the polytheists, invite them to any of three dispositions or arrangements; and if they agree to any of these, accept this and desist from any further action against them: (1) Invite them to Islam; if they agree, accept this and desist from any further action against them. (2) Then invite them to relocate from their land to the land of Muslim emigrants, and inform them that if they do so, they shall have the same rights and obligations as the emigrants have; if they refuse to relocate,

inform them that their status shall be as that of the bedouin Muslims, that they shall be subject to the same rules of God that are applied to the Believers in general. (3) If they reject these arrangements, petition them to pay the tax on religious minorities; if they agree, accept this and desist from any further action against them; if they refuse, seek God's aid and fight them. And if you lay siege to a fortress and they express their wish that you grant them a treaty of protection guaranteed by God and His Messenger, do not grant them protection guaranteed by God or His Messenger. Rather, grant them protection guaranteed by you and your companions. For if you fail to fulfill your guarantee to protect them, this will be less serious than failing to fulfill the guarantee of God and His Messenger. Likewise, if you lay siege to a fortress and they ask you for a settlement according to the rule of God, do not grant them a settlement according to the rule of God. Rather, grant them a settlement according to your ruling; for you do not know if the settlement you reach will be in full accord with the rule of God or not.'"[39]

132 It is related in the *Ṣaḥīḥ* collection of al-Bukhārī on the authority of al-Mughīrah b. Shu'bah, that he said to the soldiers of Khosrow on the day of Nahrawand: "The Messenger of our Lord commanded us to fight you until you worship God alone or you pay the tax on religious minorities."[40]

133 Thus, the Prophet• obligated us to accept the tax on religious minorities whenever they agree and desire to pay it, and he commanded us to desist thereupon from any further action against them. In other words, it is forbidden to fight them whenever they desire to pay the tax on religious minorities. Imām 'Alī said, "They simply pay the tax on religious minorities in order to render their blood and property as our blood and our property."

134 Shaykh al-Ḥaṣkafī said, regarding the definition of *jizyah:* "In lexical terms it is a recompense, because it offsets killing." Ibn 'Ābidīn said in his supercommentary: "That is, it substitutes and suffices in place of killing. Thus, whenever a non-Muslim agrees to it, he becomes exempt from being killed." Al-Shirāzī said: "Whoever seeks a contract of protection, among those whose Unbelief may be tolerated in exchange for the tax on religious minorities, must be granted such, based on His* statement {*Fight those who do not believe in God and the Last Day and do not forbid what God and His Messenger have forbidden and do not practice the religion of truth among those who have been given The Book, until they offer up the tax on religious minorities in a state of humble submission*}" [9:29].

135 And it was stated verbatim in the book, *Tanwīr al-Abṣār* and its commentary, *al-Durr al-Mukhtār:* {If we lay siege to them, we invite them to Islam. If they accept} then we proceed accordingly. {Otherwise, we move to the tax on religious minorities} if this proves to be legally sanctioned, as will be discussed. {If they accept this, then they have the right we have} to fairness {and the duty we have} to be fair. Ibn 'Ābidīn stated in his supercommentary: "His statement {if this proves to be legally sanctioned}, that is, that they are neither apostates nor among the Arabian polytheists. And his statement {they have the rights we have to fairness, etc.}, that is, to conduct their affairs with justice and fairness, on the one hand, and to demand fairness and justice, on the other." He added in the book *al-Manḥ:* "What is meant here is that they have the right over us and we over them that if we act in a manner that threatens their blood or property or they act in a manner that threatens our blood or property that they be treated in the same way as one of us who threatened the blood or property of another of us would be treated." Ṣaḥnūn said: "The tax on religious minorities is

what we take from the Unbelievers in exchange for their security and the sparing of their blood, while allowing them to remain in a state of Unbelief."

136 Now, if it is said: But in our times, when states neither demand of the People of the Book living in their jurisdictions that they pay the tax on religious minorities nor extend to them any contracts of protection, what should be the relationship between the Islamist movements and the People of the Book? Should they fight them until they agree to pay the tax on religious minorities? Or should they simply leave them alone, or what?

137 We respond: As for individuals or groups who have no means of independently extracting the tax on religious minorities nor of independently extending contracts of protection, there is no way to advocate that they do such. For contracts of protection entail mutual obligations on both sides. And individuals cannot fulfill these. Shaykh al-Maḥallī (d. 864/1459) said in his commentary on al-Nawawī's *Minhāj al-Ṭālibīn:* "Section. {We are obligated to desist from any action against them} in that we undertake no actions against their lives or property {and we indemnify what we destroy of theirs in the way of life or property}, that is, anyone among us who destroys any of this indemnifies them for it {and to defend them against hostile enemies} whether they, that is, the People of the Book, reside in the lands of Islam or in their own lands." Shaykh Shihāb al-Dīn said in his supercommentary: "His statement {and to defend them against hostile enemies} this applies to specific enemies as well as others, including other Muslims and protected religious minorities. And were we to stipulate that we not be held responsible for defending them against hostile enemies, while they reside in our lands or in a place where their enemy would have to cross our lands to get to them, this stipu-

lation would invalidate the contract of protection. Otherwise, it would not. And during any period during which we do not defend them, there is no tax on religious minorities imposed upon them, given this unfulfilled obligation."

138 We may deduce from this that those groups working for the cause of Islam in lands that do not rule according to the religious law of Islam and do not impose the tax on religious minorities upon the People of the Book have no right to ratify any contract of protection with the People of the Book. For there is no way that they will be able to defend them. And as long as this remains the case, they have no right to demand from them the tax on religious minorities. And as long as the tax on religious minorities cannot be paid because of an inability on the part of the Believers, it is not permissible to fight the People of the Book for not paying the tax on religious minorities. To whom will they pay this tax? If they take it to the governing powers, the latter will say: "We do not want this from you." If they come to us with it, we will say, "We will not accept this from you because we can neither protect nor defend you." And if we try to take it from them despite our inability to protect them, the religious law will prevent us from doing so.

139 Al-Shirāzī said: "It is incumbent upon the leader of the Muslims to protect them and restrain those who seek to do them harm—Muslims and non-Muslims alike—as he must seek the release of those among them who have been taken prisoners of war, along with the return of whatever property has been taken from them, whether they live alongside the Muslims or reside in a separate polity of their own. For they pay the tax on religious minorities in exchange for their preservation and the preservation of their property. And if there is no defense, that is, of them, to the point that an entire fiscal year passes, no tax on religious minori-

ties can be imposed on them for that year. For the tax on religious minorities is in exchange for protection, which has not obtained. Thus, it cannot be imposed in exchange for such."

Impediment Nine

The Invitation to Islam Having Not Reached a People

140 On the authority of Buraydah°, who said: "Whenever the Messenger of God• appointed a general over a battalion or army, he would exhort him to be mindful of God regarding his personal conduct and to do good by the Muslims under his charge. And he would say to him, 'When you meet your enemy among the polytheists, invite them to one of three dispositions: Invite them to Islam, and if they agree to this, accept it and desist from any further action against them.'"[41] Thus the Prophet• obligated his generals to extend the invitation to Islam before engaging in any fighting. Ibn Qudāmah° (d. 620/1223) said in his book *al-Muqni'*, "Whomever has not received the invitation is to be invited to Islam before being fought. And it is not permissible to fight them before this invitation has been extended."

141 Al-Shirāzī said in his book *al-Muhadhdhab*, "And if the enemy is among those who have not received the invitation, it is not permissible to fight them until they are invited to Islam. For, they cannot be obligated to embrace Islam before receiving knowledge of it, the proof of this being His* statement {*We would not engage in punishment before sending forth a messenger*} [17:15]. And it is not permissible to fight them over that to which they have no obligation." Al-Khiraqī (d. 334/945?) said, "Idolaters are to be invited to Islam before prosecuting any war against them."

Ibn Qudāmah added in his commentary: "If we find among them some who have not received the invitation, they are to be invited before they are fought. Likewise, if we find among the People of the Book some who have not received the invitation, they are to be invited before being fought."

142 It is stated in *Tanwīr al-Abṣār* and its commentary *al-Durr al-Mukhtār:* "{It is not} permissible for us {to fight those who have not received the invitation} according to the proper phonetics of 'invitation' {to Islam}. And though Islam as a general matter has become widely known in the world today, in the East as well as in the West, there remains, without doubt, some on God's green earth who have no awareness of it. And even if they might be aware of Islam, this does not automatically extend to an awareness of the tax on religious minorities. Thus, it is stated in the book *al-Tatarkhāneh:* 'They should also not be fought until they are invited to accept the tax on religious minorities.'"

143 Ibn 'Ābidīn stated in his supercommentary: His statement "{It is not permissible for us} is because it is through the invitation that they come to know that we are not fighting them to take their money or enslave their children. And if they know this, they might respond positively to our intended goal without any fighting. Thus, it is necessary to ascertain whether or not they have this knowledge. And if the Muslim ruler fights them before extending this invitation, he incurs a sin, because this is prohibited. His statement '{should not}' carries the apparent meaning that it is not permissible, as other examples of this will demonstrate. And the point of all of this is that whoever does not receive the invitation to Islam may not be fought until after this invitation has been extended to them. And if they accept this and believe, there remains no point in launching campaigns against them. On the contrary, we

must desist from fighting them. And this is not limited to those whose original status is that of non-Muslims, but extends to others, including Muslim rebels—that is, those who revolt against a legitimate ruler without just cause—as well as apostates. Both of these groups should be invited before being fought. The invitation to rebels, however, is an invitation to return to recognizing proper authority and to the bonds of community, while the invitation to apostates is to return to their religion."

144 Shaykh al-Maḥallī said in his commentary on al-Nawawī's *Minhāj al-Ṭālibīn:* "{And he is not to fight} he being the Muslim ruler {rebels until he dispatches to them a wise and trustworthy representative who will ask them about their grievance. And if they mention an injustice} according to the proper phonetics of 'injustice' {or an ostensible pretext, he must address this. If they then persist} after this has been addressed, he is to show sincerity towards them by admonishing them and commanding them to return to recognizing his authority. {Then}, that is, if they do not return to the fold {he declares} according to the proper phonetics of 'declares,' that is, he makes known to them that he will wage {war against them}. Shaykh Shihāb al-Dīn said in his supercommentary: His statement, '{The Muslim ruler is not to fight}, that is, it is not permissible for him, and thus it is forbidden for him until he dispatches this representative to them.'"

145 Al-Shirāzī stated in his book *al-Muhadhdhab,* speaking about apostates: "Is it obligatory or simply recommended that they be asked to repent? There are two opinions. The second is that it is obligatory, based on what has been narrated to the effect that 'Umar b. al-Khaṭṭāb° was informed that the city of Tustur had fallen to the Muslims. He asked, 'Is there any other news from that distant outpost?' They said, 'Yes, a man apostatized and joined

the polytheists. So we seized him and executed him.' He replied, 'Should you not have sequestered him in a house for three days, locked its door, and fed him a loaf of bread each day while asking him to repent? If he repented, all would be well and fine; if not, *then* you would execute him? My Lord, I did not witness this, nor did I order it, nor did it please me when it reached my attention.'[42] And were asking for repentance not obligatory, 'Umar° would not have absolved himself of their action."

Impediment Ten

Contracting Peace Treaties

146 Shaykh al-Ḥaṣkafī said in his commentary on *Tanwīr al-Abṣār:* "{And peace treaties are permissible} that stipulate abandoning jihad {against them in exchange for money} from them or from us {if that serves a benefit} based on His* statement {*And if they incline towards peace, incline you too towards it*} [8:61]." Ibn 'Ābidīn added in his supercommentary: "According to unanimous consensus, this verse is qualified by the necessity of identifying a communal interest (as the basis of such a treaty). The author of *al-Durr al-Mukhtār* said in his commentary on *Tanwīr al-Abṣār,* speaking about rebels: '{If they request to be allowed to lay down their arms, this is to be granted} to them {if it is good for the Muslims} as in the case of non-Muslim combatants.' And regarding apostates, he said, '{And} we agree to peace with {apostates if they seize control over a land and this land becomes an Abode of War}, and this is good (for the Muslims) {in exchange for no money. Otherwise} if they do not seize control over a land {we do not} agree to such a peace; for in doing so we effectively endorse the apostates' apostasy. And this is not permissible.'"

147 The point in all of this is that contracting peace treaties between the various warring factions is permissible. And once such a treaty has been ratified, fighting becomes prohibited, be this treaty temporary or unlimited in duration. Abū al-Khaṭṭāb° (d. 510/1116) said: "The most apparent construction to be put on the position of Aḥmad b. Ḥanbal (d. 241/855), that is, regarding treaties, is that it is permissible to extend them beyond ten, that is, years, in accordance with what the Muslim ruler deems to serve the community's interest. Abū Ḥanīfa (d. 150/767) held the same opinion, based on the idea that as any contract may have a duration of ten years, this duration may also be extended, as in the case of rental contracts. And the general stipulation limiting such treaties to ten years is restricted by a consideration implicitly present in any decision to go beyond this, namely that the interest served by extending such treaties may be greater than the interest served by war."

148 Al-Qurṭubī said in his exegetical work, *al-Jāmiʿ li Aḥkām al-Qurʾān:* "If some interest accrues to Muslims in contracting a peace treaty, for example, a benefit they derive or a harm they avert, there is nothing wrong with their initiating such a treaty, whenever they find a need for it. Ibn Ḥabīb (d. 238/853) related on the authority of Mālik°: 'It is permissible to enter into peace treaties with the polytheists for one, two, or three years, or even longer.'"

149 Ibn Qayyim al-Jawzīyah (d. 751/1350) said: "The permissibility of the Muslim ruler's initiating efforts to reach a peace treaty with the enemy, if he sees this as serving the interests of the Muslims, is not contingent upon the enemy's having expressed such a desire first. Indeed, even peace settlements with polytheists that

include some measure of inequity inflicted upon the Muslims are permissible, if the interest served thereby is preponderant or it averts an even greater evil. For this is simply a matter of repelling a greater harm by tolerating a lesser one." He added: "And in the account, that is, of Khaybar,[43] there is proof that it is permissible to contract unconditional peace treaties with no time limit whatever, in fact that the Muslim ruler may extend it for as long as he wishes. And there is absolutely nothing that occurred subsequent to this that might abrogate this ruling. Thus, the correct position is that this is permissible and valid. Al-Shāfiʿī (204/819–20) stated this explicitly in the narration of his teachings by al-Muzanī (d. 264/878), as have other Imāms. And among those who have also stated this is Ibn Taymīya°."

150 Ibn Qudāmah al-Maqdisī (d. 620/1223) stated: "Whenever a peace treaty is contracted, it must be fulfilled, based on His* statement {*O you who believe, fulfill your agreements*} [5:1]." He added: "And if the Muslim ruler contracts a peace treaty, he must protect the contracting party from both the Muslims and his non-Muslim protected minorities. For he has guaranteed their safety from everyone in his jurisdiction and under his sovereignty, just as he guarantees the safety of everyone in his jurisdiction from them. And whoever among the Muslims or the non-Muslim minorities destroys anything of the contracting party must indemnify the latter for this." He also said: "If the Muslim ruler contracts a peace treaty and then dies or is removed from office, this treaty is not thereby rendered defunct. Rather, whoever succeeds him must fulfill it. For the Muslim ruler contracted this on the basis of his legally sanctioned informed discretion. It is thus not permissible to overturn this on the basis of the informed discretion of someone else."

Conclusion

151 As part of the Islamic movement, it is incumbent that the goal before us toward which we strive be clear. And we must evaluate every step we take in light of the extent to which it contributes to the realization of this goal. Our apex goal is that with which all of the prophets came to their people: *Worship God. You have no god other than Him* [23:32]. Our goal, then, is to bring the people to the worship of their Lord, in other words, to guide humanity. And we must have the necessary courage to undertake any decision we see as contributing to the realization of this goal.

152 But it is also necessary that we have the requisite courage to abandon any decision we see as placing distance between us and this goal. Similarly, we must have the even greater courage to turn away from any decisions or actions that some of us may have actually embarked upon, it now being clear that these do not assist us in arriving at our aforementioned goal, that is, guiding humanity. And it is not the least bit courageous for us to leave the mill of war turning between the sons of our homeland, while we are certain that before it grinds to powder their skulls and bones it will grind to powder the very call to this religion. Rather, courage is what the Prophet• demonstrated when he saw that the interest of the Community lay in abandoning war against Quraysh, thus agreeing to a peace treaty with them, to the point that ʿUmar protested, "Why do we subject ourselves to humiliation in our religion?"[44] And it was from his• courage that Khālid b. al-Walīd learned and thus withdrew the Muslim army on the day of Muʾtah, abandoning the battle, to the point that some Muslims shouted at him and his army, "Runaways, runaways!"[45]

153 It is from our Prophet• that we have received our teachings

and from him that we learn our lessons. And it on this basis that we issued this Initiative to Stop the Armed Confrontations in Egypt.

154 Yes, some of our brethren will chide us, saying, "What about the inoperative *sharī'ah* and the ruler who does not rule by what God has revealed?" We will say:

155 First: The fighting that raged was not for the purpose of reinstating the *sharī'ah;* nor was it an act of revolting against the ruler for the purpose of ousting him. Rather, it was an expression of protest against injustices that had befallen us, and an attempt to retrieve lost rights.

156 Second, and this is the more important point: What we have cited above as impediments to fighting, whenever these impediments occur they render fighting unlawful and prohibited, whether this fighting takes the form of revolting against a ruler, battling injustices, or any other cause. As long as this revolt proves useless, does not realize any goal, and does not obliterate any harm—rather it entails harms and tribulations the extent of which only God can assess—and at the same time it leads to blocking all paths to calling people to God, let alone the destruction of large groups of those who call to the path of God, who are themselves unable to engage in this fighting and have no power to do so, being individuals strewn about the country, easily eradicated if they should all decide to fight—by what proof, after all of this, could you say to them, "Spill your blood and spill the blood of your countrymen?"

157 Yes, these acts of violence must stop, having reached the point of bringing some of us to armed campaigns. For the religious law commands us to stop them. And whoever might hold us in contempt, let him do so. For, for not for a single day have we hoped to attain the approval of the people, such that we would fear their contempt today. And whoever might find herein a good

opportunity to attack us, let him do so. For this will not be the first time that we have been attacked; nor will it be the last time, God willing, that God comes to our defense. And whoever among our brethren finds that our point of view brings misgivings to his heart, let him not be saddened. Nor will we be saddened; nor will we be angered, even if it is said to us what 'Umar said to the Prophet: "Why do we subject ourselves to humiliation in our religion?" For to say this here is to adduce this statement out of place, as there is a world of difference between the two situations. Nevertheless, we will cite for them—and remind them in this context—of the Prophet's• response to 'Umar°: "I am the servant of God, and He will never bring me to ruin."

158 By God, we hope that we too will enjoy an ample share as referents of this noble statement and that our efforts will engender the desired multiplier effect among our brethren. We ask God* not to bring us to ruin and not to bring our brethren to ruin. And God Almighty speaks the truth: *It is not God's way to bring your faith to ruin. Verily, God is indeed kind and merciful to the people* [2:143].

Appendix

Shaykh Yūsuf al-Qaraḍāwī stated: There are universal precepts and general juristic principles that the scholars of Islam have established, based on the textual sources of the *sharī'ah* and an inductive reading of its individual rules. These precepts and principles have become thus basic sources for legislation that are invoked and relied upon and from which guidance is sought in promulgating laws or issuing *fatwā*s or binding judicial decrees.

Among these precepts are: "the preservation of interests"; "the avoidance of harm takes precedence over the procurement of interest"; "a lesser interest may be forfeited to procure a greater one"; and "a restricted harm may be tolerated to avert a widespread harm."

Whenever these interests collide with countervailing harms or these benefits with countervailing detriments, the established approach is to look to the magnitude of the interest and harm in question, along with its impact and extent. Negligible harms will be pardoned to protect greater interests, and temporary harms will be pardoned to protect more permanent and long-term interests. Likewise, a harm is to be tolerated—even a great harm—if its eradication is likely to lead to an even greater harm. And under normal circumstances, the avoidance of harm is given priority over the procurement of interest.

Now, it is not so important that we recognize this approach to understanding the law in theory. What is important—and vitally so—is that we adopt it in practice. For many of the causes of conflict between the various factions working for Islam revert to this very calculus:

1. Is it acceptable to contract alliances with non-Islamic forces?
2. Is it acceptable to contract settlements and truces with governments that are not committed to Islam?
3. Can one participate in a government that is not purely Islamic, in a context where the constitution contains loopholes or provisions with which we are not fully satisfied?
4. Do we enter into oppositional coalitions made up of various parties for the purpose of toppling a corrupt, tyrannical regime?
5. Do we seek to establish Islamic economic institutions despite the worldwide dominance of the secular, usury-based system?
6. Do we permit Islamically oriented persons to work in banks and other usury-based institutions? Or do we seek to empty these of all religiously committed people?

The Difficulty of Practicing and Applying This in Practical Life

Establishing principles is easy. Practicing them, however, is difficult, because the jurisprudence of prioritizing harms and interests weighs heavily upon the laity and their like, including those who have the ability to sow confusion on the slightest provocation. Indeed, the eminent scholar al-Mawdūdī, along with his group, faced much grief when he deemed—in light of this jurisprudence of prioritizing harms and interests—the election of Fāṭimah Jināḥ (Jinnah) to be less harmful than that of Ayyūb Khān. Indeed, they unleashed hell on him via the hadith, "No people who consign their affair to a woman shall prosper." Now, shall a people who consign their affair to a brutal dictator prosper? They will not. And true jurisprudence here is to look at which is the lesser evil and which the lighter harm and then to tolerate the lesser for the sake of avoiding the greater. And the most important things upon which the jurisprudence of prioritizing harms and interests is based are:

1. Prioritizing the various legally recognized interests, benefits or goods.
2. Prioritizing, in like fashion, the various legally recognized harms, disadvantages, and evils.
3. Prioritizing, as well, the various interests, benefits, goods, and evils where they collide and conflict with each other.

Prioritizing Interests

Under the first category, "interests," we find that the interests that are recognized by the religious law are not of a single priority. Rather, as established by the scholars of legal theory, they fall into three basic levels of priority: vital interests (*ḍārūrīyāt*); valued interests (*ḥājīyāt*); and supplementary interests (*taḥsīnīyāt*).

Now, vital interests are those without which life cannot be sustained. Valued interests are those without which life can be sustained but with undue hardship and constriction. Supplementary interests are those things that embellish and beautify life and are thus customarily referred to as "complements." In this light, the jurisprudence of prioritizing harms and interests, and thus the jurisprudence of setting priorities, demands of us that we recognize:

1. The precedence of vital interests over valued interests and, a fortiori, over supplementary interests, and of valued interests over supplementary interests and complements.
2. That as vital interests are themselves of varying levels of priority, they are, as the scholars have mentioned, five in number: (1) religion; (2) life ; (3) progeny; (4) sanity;[1] (5) property; and some add a sixth, dignity.

Now, religion is the first and most important interest, taking precedence over all other vital interests, including life, just as life takes precedence over everything else. And in prioritizing interests, we give priority to those that are certain to obtain over those that are only suspected of obtaining or whose occurrence is merely imagined as a possibility. Great interests are given precedence over small ones. And the interests of groups are given precedence over those of individuals. The interests of the many are given precedence over the interests of the few. And permanent interests are given precedence over passing or terminal ones. Core, fundamental interests are given precedence over cosmetic or marginal interests. And the strong interests of the future are given precedence over weak, immediate interests.

During the Treaty of Ḥudaybīya, we saw the Prophet• give preponderance to future, core, fundamental interests over cosmetic interests and considerations to which some people cling so desperately today.

Indeed, he accepted conditions that one might think at first blush constituted an affront to the Muslim community or an acceptance of inferiority on their part: He accepted the phrase, "In the name of God the All-Merciful, the Mercy-Giving," with which treaties had traditionally been commenced, being removed and substituted with, "In Your name, O God." And he accepted that the attribution of prophethood, "Muḥammad the Messenger of God," which had been inextricably attached to his noble name, be removed, settling in its stead for, "Muḥammad the son of 'Abd Allāh." All of this in order to arrive at the truce that would allow him to devote all of his efforts to spreading The Call and addressing the rulers of the earth. It is thus no wonder that the Qur'ān called this truce "a manifest victory". And examples of this type are numerous.

Prioritizing Harms and Detriments

Under the second category, "harms and detriments," we find that they are of varying degrees, just like interests. Harms that undermine a vital interest are not like harms that undermine valued interests, which are not like harms that undermine supplementary interests. And harms that affect property are not like harms that affect life, which are not like harms that affect religion and creed. Moreover, harms or detriments vary in magnitude, impact, and degree of seriousness. And on this basis, the jurists have established a number of calibrating precepts for the most important rulings affected in this regard. Among these are:

1. There shall be no harm and no reciprocal harm.
2. Harms shall be removed to the extent possible.
3. Harms shall not be removed through a like or greater harm.
4. The least harm and the lesser evil shall be indulged (under necessity).

5. The lesser harm is to be tolerated in order to avoid the greater harm.
6. The restricted harm is to be tolerated in order to avoid the unrestricted harm.

Prioritizing Interests and Harms Where They Collide

Whenever an interest and a harm or a detriment and a benefit gather in a single affair, one must prioritize. And consideration must go to that quality that is most preponderant and most prevalent. Indeed, the quality that is most prevalent is treated as if it characterizes the thing as a whole. Thus, if the harm attending a particular act is more prevalent or preponderant than the benefit or interest attending it, one must move to prevent the harm, given its relative preponderance. And in this case, no consideration will be given to the small amount of benefit that might otherwise obtain. This, in fact, is how the Qur'ān proceeds in the matter of wine-drinking and games of chance, in response to those who asked about these: *They ask you about wine drinking and games of chance. Say, in them is great vice, along with benefits for people; but their vice is greater than their benefit* [2:219].

Conversely, if the benefit is greater and more preponderant, the action is to be allowed and considered legitimate, and the small amount of harm that might obtain is to be ignored. And among the important precepts in this context is, "The avoidance of harm shall take precedence over the procurement of benefit." This, however, must be brought to completion by another precept, namely, "Small amounts of harm are to be pardoned in the face of great benefit, transient harms are to be pardoned in the face of permanent benefits, and no benefit whose occurrence is known with certainty is to be forfeited in the face of a harm that is simply imagined as a possibility."

This Jurisprudence of Prioritization is enormously important in real life, especially in the area of *sharī'ah*-based politics. For the latter is founded fundamentally on the basis of observing this very jurisprudence. And this is extremely important for the Jurisprudence of Priorities.

(Regarding these principles see, *al-Ashbāh wa al-naẓā'ir* of Ibn Nujaym, the section on legal precepts (*qawā'id*). See also *Uṣūl al-tashrī'*, by al-Khuḍarī.)

Notes

Preface

1. See, e.g., Islamopedia Online, www.islamopediaonline.com/news/jamaa-islamiya-condemns-attacks-targeting-military-forces-sinai; and Ahram Online, "Al-Gamaa al-Islamiya Denies Role in Church Attacks," http://english.ahram.org.eg/NewsContent/1/0/79134/Egypt/0/AlGamaa-AlIslamiya-denies-role-in-church-attacks.aspx; and Islamopedia Online, "Jama'a al'Islamiya: Infringing on Christians [*sic*] Live or Property Is a Sin," www.islamopediaonline.org/news/jamaa-al-islamiya-infringing-christians-lives-or-property-sin (all accessed January 16, 2014).

2. See, e.g., the translated text below, §7, 40–44; *also Ḥurmat al-ghulūw fī al-dīn wa takrīr al-muslimīn* (Cairo: Maktabat al-Turāth al-Islāmī, 2002), 8ff.

Introduction

1. By "allies," I am referring, not to those who subscribe to a common political agenda with the West, but to those who reject the proposition that Islam and Western-*cum*-American civilization cannot peacefully coexist. As such, they reject unwarranted violence against

America and the West in the name of Islam. Such interlocutors would seem to play an increasingly valuable role today, given such sentiments as those expressed by Republican presidential candidate Mitt Romney during the third presidential debate on October 22, 2012. Speaking of America's strained and uncertain relationship with the Muslim world, he opined, "We will not be able to kill our way out of this mess."

2. See his *Security First: Towards a Muscular and Moral Foreign Policy* (New Haven: Yale University Press, 2007), xiv–xvi. See also, however, my partial review of this work, "Between Preachers and Warriors," *American Behavioral Scientist* 52, no. 9 (May 2008): 1377–86.

3. By "radical, jihadist" I refer to those for whom violence is the primary medium of exchange, the sanctity of innocent human life, Muslim and non-Muslim alike, being easily and often unscrupulously sacrificed to the pursuit of their would-be Islamic cause.

4. On the size of the organization, M. M. Aḥmad notes that the *Gamāʿah* constituted "the largest violent, terrorist organization in Egypt and the Arab world. See his *Muʾāmarah am murājaʿah: Ḥiwār maʿa qiyādat al-taṭarruf fī sijn al-ʿaqrab* (Cairo: Dār al-Shurūq, 1423/2003), 174. Meanwhile, ʿA. al-Fiqī places the number of incarcerated members at thirteen thousand. See his "al-Jamāʿah al-islāmīyah: al-Tawajjuhāt al-ijtimāʿīyah baʿd al-sujūn," in *Rāʾiḥat al-bārūd: Murājaʿāt al-jamāʿah al-islāmīyah fī miṣr* (Dubai: Markaz al-Misbār li al-Dirāsāt wa al-Buḥūth, 2011), 314. Kamāl al-Saʿīd Ḥabīb, a prominent member of the early coalition (see below in this introduction) who spent time in prison with *Gamāʿah* leaders following Sadat's assassination, places the number back in the 1980s "beyond fifteen thousand." See his "al-Ākhar fī fiqh al-jamāʿah al-islāmīyah qabl al-murājaʿah wa baʿdahā," in *Rāʾiḥat al-bārūd,* 153. And in a similar vein, O. Ashour reports that the group's reform efforts "took around 15,000 to 20,000 IG [*Gamāʿah*] militants away from the Salafi-Jihadi camp currently led by al-Qaʿida." See his, "Lions Tamed? An Inquiry into

the Causes of De-Radicalization of Armed Islamist Movements; The Case of the Egyptian Islamic Group," *Middle East Journal* 61, no. 4 (Autumn 2007): 596–97. Elsewhere in the same article, Ashour cites "semi-official sources" that put the number of imprisoned *Gamāʿah* members at fifteen thousand. See "Lions," 616. Another Egyptian scholar, Salwā al-ʿAwwā, puts the number of incarcerated members at thirty thousand! See her *al-Jamāʿah al-islāmīyah al-musallaḥah fī miṣr: 1974–2004* (Cairo: Maktabat al-Shurūq al-Dawlīyah, 2006), 32, 143.

5. See, however, Omar Ashour, *De-Radicalization of Jihadists: Transforming Armed Islamist Movements* (New York: Routledge, 2009); O. Ashour, "Lions Tamed?" 596–625. Ashour's analyses, however, are primarily sociological and political and do not seek to examine the actual arguments adduced by the *Gamāʿah* nor explore their broader implications. Other studies include J. Toth, "Islamism in Southern Egypt: A Case Study of a Radical Movement," *International Journal of Middle East Studies* 35, no. 4 (2003): 547–72; R. Meijer, "Commanding Right and Forbidding Wrong as a Principle for Social Action: The Case of the Egyptian al-Jamaʿa al-Islamiyya," in *Global Salafism: Islam's New Religious Movement,* ed. R. Meijer (New York: Columbia University Press, 2009), 189–220. While many studies associate the *Gamāʿah* with "Salafism" in ways that do not seem accurate or consistent, Meijer appears to detect this problem, occasionally using such terms as "semi-Salafī" or "Salafī bent." See "Commanding," 191, 217. On the one hand, the "Salafī" designation might draw some justification from *Gamāʿah* leaders' pointing to creed (*ʿaqīdah*) as one of the differences between them and the Muslim Brotherhood, the latter allegedly allowing into their ranks persons with "corrupted theological beliefs." See K. Zuhdī et al., *Istrātijīyah wa tafjīrāt al-qāʿidah al-akhṭāʾ wa al-akhṭār* (Cairo: Maktabat al-Turāth al-Islāmī, 2004), 344. On the other hand, identifying "commanding good and forbidding wrong" as a specifically Salafī principle seems problematic, as this can be traced

all the way back to third/ninth century Mu'tazilites and their famous Five Cardinal Principles (*al-uṣūl al-khams*). It may be more simply that the term "Salafī" has come to operate as a catchall in modern Egypt (and beyond) for those displaying a certain 'style' of Islamic belief, practice and activism, despite the fact that these groups do not identify with each other. Back in the early 1980s, such persons might have been referred to as "Sunnīs," e.g., "*wāḥid sunnī,*" despite the fact that the entire country was overwhelmingly Sunni.

6. This is not to mention the numerous statements on the *Gamā'ah*'s official website: www.egyig.com. According to al-'Awwā, *al-Jamā'ah,* 59, this website has been in operation since 2006.

7. Their understanding of *sharī'ah* at the time was limited, however, to *fiqh,* with no consideration or recognition of *siyāsah,* i.e., the powers of discretion traditionally ceded to the Muslim state, on the basis of which it might legitimately modify or even suspend the application of *sharī'ah* rules, according to circumstances. Interestingly, the *Gamā'ah* would eventually evolve into a recognition of precisely this kind of legitimately state-owned prerogative. See below in this introduction. On *siyāsah* in general, see the important work of Frank Vogel, *Islamic Law and Legal System* (Leiden: E. J. Brill, 2000).

8. The work itself was of limited distribution. See, however, Ni'mat Allāh Junaynah, *Tanẓīm al-jihād: Hal huwa al-badīl al-islāmī fī miṣr?* (Cairo: Dār al-Ḥurrīyah li al-Ṣiḥāfah wa al-Ṭibā'ah wa al-Nashr, 1409/1988), 223–73, for a reproduction of the entire text in Arabic. For an English translation, see Johannes J. G. Jansen, *The Neglected Duty: The Creed of Sadat's Assassins and Islamic Resurgence in the Middle East* (New York: Macmillan, 1986), 159–234. Jansen notes that several editions of this tract were published, not all of them entirely congruent. In his view, the best of these is the one issued in 1984 by the Egyptian Ministry of Awqāf, which is apparently what Junaynah relied upon in her reproduction. See *The Neglected Duty,* 3.

9. See, e.g., D. J. Sullivan and S. Abed-Kotob, *Islam in Contemporary Egypt: Civil Society vs. the State* (Boulder, CO: Lynne Rienner Publishers, 1999), 79, where the original *Tanẓīm al-Jihād* is said to have simply expanded in 1979 under the leadership of Faraj.

10. See ʻAbd al-Munʻim Munīb, *Dalīl al-ḥarakāt al-islāmīyah al-miṣrīyah* (Cairo: Maktabat Madbūlī, 2010), 6.

11. See ibid., 85.

12. See Junaynah, *Tanẓīm,* 147–222.

13. Ḥabīb actually became the leader of this group following the deportation in 1979 of its original leader, Muḥammad Sālim al-Raḥḥ āl, a Palestinian with a Jordanian passport studying at al-Azhar. See Junaynah, *Tanẓīm,* 101–2; Munīb, *Dalīl,* 90. According to al-ʻAwwā, however, al-Raḥḥāl's group did not actually join the *Tanẓīm al-Jihād* coalition until they landed in prison after Sadat's assassination. See her *al-Jamāʻah,* 21.

14. See Munīb, *Dalīl,* 72–91.

15. Al-ʻAwwā, basing her research partly on interviews with *Gamāʻah* leaders and members, traces the beginnings of the group back to the late 1960s, though from that time into the 1970s it underwent several name-changes, eventually settling on *al-Gamāʻah al-Islāmīyah* in 1973, reportedly through inspiration drawn from the books of the Indian-cum-Pakistani thinker Abū al-Aʻlā al-Mawdūdī, who founded *Jamat-i-Islami* in 1941. See al-ʻAwwā, *al-Jamāʻah,* 68. Meanwhile, Muḥammad Abū Zayd suggests that it was, ironically, Sadat who authorized and supported the development of religious movements on university campuses to offset the influence of his leftist opposition. The *Gamāʻah* eventually—and inadvertently—emerged out of this. See "al-Jamāʻah al-islāmīyah al-miṣrīyah: al-Bidāyah wa al-nihāyah," in *Rāʼiḥat al-bārūd,* 11–12.

16. Indeed, following the assassination of Sadat, the movement spread to every major city, including Alexandria and Cairo, outstrip-

ping the Muslim Brotherhood in Upper Egypt and becoming a major competitor in other parts of the country. See Ḥabīb, "al-Ākhar," 142–43, including notes 3 and 4.

17. A number of *Gamāʿah* members did actually join the Muslim Brotherhood, e.g., Abū al-ʿAlāʾ Māḍī and Muḥyī al-Dīn ʿĪsā. See Munīb, *Dalīl,* 144. In fact, according to Meijer, "Commanding," 196–97, the entire Lower Egypt faction of the group threw its lot in with the Muslim Brotherhood, prompting a split within the early *Gamāʿah.*

18. Even as the senior Islamist movement in Egypt, the Muslim Brotherhood had formally abandoned political violence as a tactic upon the release of its leaders from prison in the 1970s. See al-ʿAwwā, *al-Jamāʿah,* 24. Their new position is presumably reflected in the work of the Supreme Guide (*murshid*), Ḥasan al-Hudaybī, *Duʿāt lā quḍāt* (Preachers, Not Judges), which appeared in 1977. Aḥmad claims, however, that documents later seized from the Muslim Brotherhood indicate that all of this was merely a tactical move, following which they planned to resume their use of violence. See *Muʾāmarah,* 228–39. Later, at any rate, the *Gamāʿah* would criticize the Muslim Brotherhood's entry into politics, their willingness to make alliances with secular political parties, and their relationship with Christians. See Ḥabīb, "al-Ākhar," 153.

19. Muntaṣir al-Zayyāt, *The Road to Al-Qaeda: The Story of bin Lāden's Right-Hand Man,* trans. A. Fekry (London: Pluto Press, 2004), 33.

20. See Junaynah, *Tanẓīm,* 157–62.

21. Even here it might be noted that, according to al-ʿAwwā, a number of prominent members of *Tanẓīm al-Jihād,* including Ayman al-Ẓawāhirī, ʿAbbūd al-Zumar, and others, actually opposed the decision to kill Sadat for tactical reasons. See *al-Jamāʿah,* 97, 98.

22. See Junaynah, *Tanẓīm,* 161, 175, and passim.

23. Munīb insists that it was actually "the hawks (*al-ṣuqūr*)" Karam

Zuhdī and 'Alī al-Sharīf, who, overcome with enthusiasm upon learning of Sadat's death, exercised a bit of "intellectual and rhetorical terrorism (*irhāb fikrī wa kalāmī*)" to coerce the other leaders and members of the *Gamā'ah* into continuing with their plans to carry out the Asyūṭ mission. See *Dalīl,* 97–98.

24. These included, 'Abd al-Ḥamīd 'Abd al-Salām 'Abd al-'Āl, 'Aṭā Ṭāyil Ḥamīdah al-Raḥīl, and Ḥusayn 'Abbās Muḥammad.

25. In fact, several members of the *Gamā'ah* ended up getting shot, some were maimed by their own explosives, transport vehicles broke down, got stuck in the sand, and even ran out of gas! On these complications, see Junaynah, *Tanẓīm,* 162, 166, 170, 175, 177. Still, according to al-'Awwā, *al-Jamā'ah,* 101, 151, this mission led to the death of some one hundred people, mostly security forces.

26. See Junaynah, *Tanẓīm,* 161, 175.

27. See 'Abd al-Mun'im Munīb, *Murāja'āt al-jihādīyīn: al-Qaḍīyah al-khafīyah li murāja'āt al-jihād wa al-jamā'ah al-islāmīyah dākhila wa khārija al-sujūn* (Cairo: Maktabat Madbūlī, 2010), 8–9; Munīb, *Dalīl,* 178; al-'Awwā, *al-Jamā'ah,* 107. The general consensus seems to be that this occurred sometime between late 1983 and 1984. This may explain, at least in part, the tendency among *Tanẓīm al-Jihād* members, albeit much later, to join *al-Qā'idah.* In fact, Munīb, *Dalīl,* 110, insists that *Tanẓīm al-Jihād* members would eventually form the very backbone of *al-Qā'idah.* As for their differences, Ashour notes that three were primary: (1) disagreement over the leadership of Shaykh 'Umar 'Abd al-Raḥmān (the *Gamā'ah* being for, *Jihād* against); (2) the question of whether those who sinned out of ignorance were pardonable (*Gamā'ah*) or not (*Jihād*); and (3) whether the coalition should be involved in public preaching (*Gamā'ah*) or limit its primary focus to clandestine maneuvers to seize power (*Jihād*). See "Lions," 607–08. Meanwhile, al-'Awwā, *al-Jamā'ah,* 24, 107, adds that *Tanẓīm al-Jihād* felt that they should have a privileged place in the leadership, given

their role in the assassination of Sadat and the price that some of their members had paid for it.

28. According to al-ʻAwwā, *al-Jamāʻah,* 21, this was "after just three or four years," i.e., between 1984 and 1985. Munīb, meanwhile, sets the date of dissolution at 1986. See *Murājaʻāt,* 23.

29. Indeed, Munīb would characterize the leadership in prison as a "dictatorship" and speak of the deference granted the Consultative Council by second-tier leaders and rank-and-file members as bordering on apotheosis (*taqdīs*). See *Murājaʻāt,* 35, 240.

30. See al-ʻAwwā, *al-Jamāʻah,* 111–12; Ashour, "Lions," 610.

31. On these works and the atmosphere in which they were written, see al-ʻAwwā, *al-Jamāʻah,* 106–7; Ashour, "Lions," 609. I have altered some of Ashour's translations of titles. See also, however, al-ʻAwwā, *al-Jamāʻah,* 88, where at least one *Gamāʻah* member, Ṣafwat ʻAbd al-Ghanī, insists that there were formal writings in existence before their imprisonment. Meanwhile, first-tier leader Nājiḥ Ibrāhīm, an early veteran of the movement, states unequivocally that the *Gamāʻah* did not begin writing until after they landed in prison. See al-ʻAwwā, *al-Jamāʻah,* 106. See also Abū Zayd, "al-Jamāʻah al-islāmīyah," 20, and Ḥabīb, "al-Ākhar," 143 n. 6, for a similar view.

32. Al-ʻAwwā, *al-Jamāʻah,* 106.

33. See, e.g., al-ʻAwwā, *al-Jamāʻah,* 138–40.

34. There are conflicting opinions and reports on the death toll. According to Gilles Kepel, *Gamāʻah* activity resulted in about a thousand deaths. See *The War for Muslim Minds: Islam and the West,* trans. Pascale Ghazaleh (Cambridge, MA: Belknap Press of Harvard University Press, 2004), 82. According to Ashour, meanwhile, between 1992 and 1996 alone, between *Gamāʻah* members, Egyptian security forces, innocent bystanders and tourists, the death toll reached 1,275. See "Lions," 612. Meanwhile, Ḥasan Bakrī, *al-ʻUnf al-siyāsī fī miṣr: Asyūṭ buʼrat al-tawattur al-asbāb wa al-dawāfiʻ* (Cairo: Markaz al-Maḥ

rūsah li al-Buḥūth wa al-Tadrīb wa al-Nashr, 1996), 127, reports that between 1991 and 1994, there were 1,119 deaths among innocent civilians, not counting police or *Gamā'ah* members. For 1995, he cites 664 such deaths. (Cited in al-'Awwā, *al-Jamā'ah,* 36 n. 6.) See also the various figures cited by al-'Awwā in her charts in *al-Jamā'ah,* 223–24.

35. In 1992, they bombed the temple of Karnak in Luxor, and fired on tourist boats in al-Minyā and tourist buses near Qinā. In 1993, they assassinated the secularist Faraj Fūda, author of the book *al-Ḥaqīqah al-ghā'ibah* (The Neglected Truth), a clear satire on 'Abd al-Salām Faraj's *al-Farīḍah al-ghā'ibah.* In 1994, they made an attempt on Nobel laureate Najīb Maḥfūẓ, who authored belletristic works apparently critical of religion. In 1995, they launched an attack at the Egyptian Museum in *Taḥrīr* square. And in 1996, they killed some eighteen Greek tourists (whom they thought were Israeli) at a hotel near the pyramids. This is in addition to the many attacks on Coptic Christians all the way up to 1997. In his study, Abū Zayd cites some thirty-one attacks on Coptic targets that took forty-two victims, not including assassinations of Coptic clerics. See his "al-Jamā'ah al-islāmīyah," 34.

36. See note 4 above.

37. According to Egyptian law at the time, suspects could be held for a maximum of two months, after which they had to be charged or released. In 1989, however, "tough-on-extremism" minister of interior Zakī Badr innovated the practice of serially rearresting suspects on paper and thus extending their detention indefinitely. See al-'Awwā, *al-Jamā'ah,* 121–22.

38. This is according to al-'Awwā, *al-Jamā'ah,* 122. Ashour, meanwhile, gives a similar but slightly modified list. See "Lions," 611.

39. See al-'Awwā, *al-Jamā'ah,* 122–24, 152–53.

40. See ibid., 129–32. Going back to the early years of the movement, *Gamā'ah* membership was loosely distributed among three main apparatuses: (1) preaching/missionary; (2) financial; and (3) military.

Muḥyī al-Dīn was part of the preaching/missionary apparatus and was openly critical of *Gamā'ah* violence. This added to the outrage among *Gamā'ah* members upon hearing of his death.

41. Mamdūḥ 'Alī Yusuf, a second-tier field commander of the military apparatus, who actually took the audacious decision to target Minister of Interior Zakī Badr, provides insight into *Gamā'ah* rationale: "The soldier who violates a mosque; what worth is he? I mean, they'll bring a hundred soldiers in his place. The officer who came and oversaw this operation, they'll bring a hundred officers to take his place. But the one who *issued* this order, now, *that's* the one I'm looking for." See al-'Awwā, *al-Jamā'ah,* 197. (Yūsuf's response is in colloquial Egyptian Arabic.)

42. See al-'Awwā, *al-Jamā'ah,* 135. The quoted segment is in colloquial Egyptian in the original Arabic text, based on interviews with Ḥāfiẓ. Ḥāfiẓ had been imprisoned in 1981, following the assassination of Sadat. In fact, he was to be the intermediary during this operation who communicated what was going on in Cairo to the Upper Egypt faction in the south. He was released in 1992 but rearrested in 1994 and sentenced to an additional ten years. See al-'Awwā, *al-Jamā'ah,* 117.

43. Zuhdī et al., *Nahr al-dhikrāyāt: al-Murāja'āt al-fiqhīyah li al-jamā'ah al-islāmīyah* (Cairo: Maktabat al-Turāth al-Islāmī, 2003), 35. At "Lions," 611–12 n. 94, Ashour provides the details of this event: "The Dayrut events started as a dispute over a 200LE ($40 U.S.) loan between a Muslim and a Copt. The dispute led to a violent clash that left two Muslims and one Copt dead. Thinking in traditional vendetta terms that are widespread in Upper Egypt, IG members interfered to avenge the two Muslims by killing one more Copt. The intervention led to multiple clashes that left seventeen Copts dead. The security forces responded with a wide-scale crackdown that included assassinating the IG *Emir* [leader] of Dayrut, Shaykh 'Arafa al-Gami, in front of the mosque in which he had just given his Friday sermon."

44. See al-ʿAwwā, *al-Jamāʿah,* 135.

45. In a telling insight into the period, the wife of a security officer reports her daily routine of stealthily going out each morning before her husband left for work to look underneath his car for planted bombs. See al-ʿAwwā, *al-Jamāʿah,* 139.

46. These included: (1) Karam Zuhdi; (2) Nājiḥ Ibrāhīm; (3) Ḥamdī ʿAbd al-Raḥmān ʿAbd al-ʿAẓīm; (4) Fu'ād al-Dawālībī; (5) ʿAlī al-Sharīf; and (6) ʿAbbūd al-Zumar. See Aḥmad, *Mu'āmarah,* 176.

47. See al-ʿAwwā, *al-Jamāʿah,* 165.

48. It should be noted that this was actually not the first call for a cessation of violence. In 1996, e.g., *Gamāʿah* field commander (*amīr*) Khālid Ibrāhīm announced a cease-fire in Aswān. But this, like similar moves, was merely a tactical decision and did not include any ideological self-examination or reorientation by the movement as a whole. On such tactical maneuvers, see Abū Zayd, "al-Jamāʿah al-islāmīyah," 37–38; Aḥmad, *Mu'āmarah,* 176.

49. The cover and title page of *Mubādarat waqf al-ʿunf* indicate that it was authored and prepared by Usāmah Ibrāhīm Ḥāfiẓ and ʿĀṣim ʿAbd al-Mājid Muḥammad, with the six names of the remaining eight signatories-cum-Consultative Council members being listed as having "endorsed and reviewed" (*aqarrahu wa rājaʿahu*) the text.

50. The review of *Mubādarat waqf al-ʿunf* was two pages long; that of *Taslīṭ al-aḍwā' ʿalā mā waqaʿa fī al-jihād min al-akhṭā'* was seven pages long; that of *al-Nuṣḥ wa al-tabyīn fī taṣḥīḥ mafāhīm al-muḥtasibīn* was two pages long; and that of *Ḥurmat al-ghulūw fī al-dīn wa takfīr al-muslimīn* was four pages long. See Aḥmad, *Mu'āmarah,* 147–48. For reproductions of the actual reviews, see ibid., 212–26.

51. For a brief profile on these men, see my "Beyond Jihad: The New Thought of the *Gamāʿa Islāmīya,*" *Journal of Islamic Law and Culture* 11, no. 1 (March 2009): 56–57 nn. 28–35. With the exception

of Ḥamdī ʿAbd al-Raḥmān and the possible exception of Aṣim ʿAbd al-Mājid Muḥammad (whose date of release I have not been able to determine) all of these men were still in prison at the time these manifestos were published. I have placed the year of birth followed by the release date of each man beside his name, based on Abū Zayd, *al-Jamāʿah al-islāmīyah,* 21–24, and Ṣ. ʿUsaylah, "Majlis shūrā al-jamāʿah al-islāmīyah: al-nash'ah, al-tanẓīm, al-rumūz," in *Rā'iḥat al-bārūd,* 56.

52. See Junaynah, *Tanẓīm,* 158.

53. See, e.g., al-ʿAwwā, *al-Jamāʿah,* 201, 202ff., where Usāmah Ibrāhim Ḥāfiẓ, who signed all the manifestos, reports his initial rejection. One also notices that while ʿĀṣim ʿAbd al-Mājid Muḥammad, Usāmah Ibrāhīm Ḥāfiẓ, and Muḥammad ʿIṣām al-Dīn Darbālah signed all the manifestos, they did not sign the original declaration issued in 1997. On the other hand, one notes that neither Ṭāriq al-Zumar nor ʿAbbūd al-Zumar, both high-ranking members who defected from *Tanẓīm al-Jihād* and joined the *Gamāʿah* in 1991, signed the manifestos, despite the fact that ʿAbbūd al-Zumar signed the original declaration in 1997. According to Munīb, *Dalīl,* 180–81, ʿAbbūd merely supported the Initiative in its original declaration for tactical reasons, i.e., to strengthen the movement's bargaining power with the government.

54. *Nahr al-dhikrāyāt,* 7. See also Abū Zayd, *al-Jamāʿah al-islāmīyah,* 38–39, where the number of dead is placed at eighty-five.

55. See ʿAbd al-Raḥīm ʿAlī, *al-Ḥaṣād al-murr: al-Dawlah wa jamāʿāt al-ʿunf al-dīnī fī miṣr, 1971–2004* (Cairo: Markaz al-Maḥrūsah li al-Nashr wa al-Khadamāt al-Ṣaḥafīyah wa al-Maʿlūmāt, 2005), 401.

56. See, e.g., Munīb, *Murājaʿāt,* 61, where he claims that the massacre resulted in the release of some four thousand *Gamāʿah* members from prison. See also Ṭāhā's series of letters directed primarily to the movement's top brass at Munīb, *Murājaʿāt,* 55–79.

57. See *United States of America v. Ahmed Abdel SATTAR, a/k/a/*

"Abu Omar," a/k/a/ "Dr. Ahmed," Lynne Stewart, and Mohammed Yousry, Defendants, at United Settlement website, http://uniset.ca/other/cs5/395FSupp2d79.html (accessed January 20, 2014). The opinion adds, "If the [Egyptian] regime worried about anyone it is (Taha)."

58. Aḥmad, *Mu'āmarah,* 45, relates from first-tier *Gamā'ah* leader Nājiḥ Ibrāhīm that Ṭāhā was actually relieved of his leadership in the *Gamā'ah* because of his position on the Initiative. Meanwhile, Karam Zuhdī insists that Ṭāhā *resigned* after they sent word to him via "the lawyer" (which I take perhaps to have been Muntaṣir al-Zayyāt) that he must either withdraw his support for bin Lādin's *fatwā* or withdraw from the *Gamā'ah.* See *Mu'āmarah,* 50. At *Road,* 89, al-Zayyāt minimizes Ṭāhā's affiliation with Bin Lādin and suggests that he was actually duped into both signing the '*fatwā*' and joining the International Front. Meanwhile, Ashour, "Lions," 617, writes: "The historical leaders sent Taha a letter through one of their lawyers demanding his immediate withdrawal from the Front. Taha withdrew one week after the declaration, but the historical leaders sacked him from his position and appointed Mustafa Hamza, former head of the military wing (1995–1998) instead." Interestingly, Zuhdī and another member of the Historical Leadership, 'Iṣām Darbālah, are said to have traced Ṭāhā's moves to "a 'trap' planned by their rivals from al-Jihad." See "Lions," 617 n. 126. Meanwhile, al-'Awwā, *al-Jamā'ah,* 179, claims that Ṭāhā eventually came around to supporting the Initiative by 1999, while Ashour insists that at the time of his writing (2007) the Historical Leaders were still trying to convince him of its Islamic legitimacy. See Ashour, "Lions," 617 n. 127.

59. Incidentally, Munīb, *Murāja'āt,* 8–9, criticizes the Historical Leadership for trying to play down Ṭāhā's stature within the *Gamā'ah* in order to play down the importance of his opposition to the Initiative. In fact, Munīb insists, Ṭāhā had an undeniably rightful claim to being part of the "Historical Leadership," inasmuch as it was he who

virtually singlehandedly brought the *Gamā'ah* back to life following its near collapse during the early years of its leadership's imprisonment.

60. Rushdī, a former field commander for Asyūṭ and al-Islāmbūlī, a former member of the Consultative Council, both resigned from the *Gamā'ah* in protest over the Initiative. Others, e.g., Muḥammad Khalīl al-Ḥukāymah, a second-tier leader from Aswān, not only resigned but publicly announced his joining *al-Qā'idah.* See Ashour, "Lions," 617 n. 127. In fact, al-Ḥukāymah originally announced his dissent in the name of *al-Gamā'ah al-Islāmīyah al-Thābitūn 'alā al-'Ahd* (The Islamic Group Who Holds True to Its Original Pledge). He was opposed by the *Gāmā'ah* leadership, however, and forced to change his affiliation to *Qā'idat al-Jihād al-Thābitūn 'alā al-'Ahd.* See Sa'īd, "*al-Ākhar*," 159.

61. *Mubādarah,* 6. Meanwhile, the group of scholars who authored *Dalīl al-ḥarakāt al-islāmīyah fī al-'ālam,* 3rd ed., ed. Ḍiyā' Rashwān et al., vol. 1 (2006), 277, give October 1998 as the date of full agreement. See, however, 'Alī, *al-Ḥaṣād al-murr,* 399–400, where he cites a communiqué apparently issued by second-tier field commanders, dated March 24, 1999, in which they affirm that *all* units of the *Gamā'ah,* both in and outside of Egypt, declare their commitment to abiding by the Initiative, in compliance with the directive of [Sh] Dr. 'Umar 'Abd al-Raḥmān. See, however, below on Shaykh 'Umar's mildly protean position.

62. "Lions," 613, 617. See below, however, where the reasons for Shaykh 'Umar 'Abd al-Raḥmān's withdrawal of support in 1999 suggest that all skirmishes had not yet come to a complete end.

63. See *Mubādarah,* 5.

64. In fact, according to the indictment of New York attorney Lynne Stewart, U.S. government sources discovered that on March 9, 1999, Shaykh 'Umar sent word to Rifā'ī Ṭāhā instructing him to abide by the Initiative and not to do anything else without first informing him. The Stewart indictment is available on Findlaw, at http://news.findlaw.com/hdocs/docs/terrorism/uslstwrt111903sind.html (accessed January 28, 2014)

65. In *Dalīl al-ḥarakāt al-islāmīyah fī al-ʿālam,* 275, 277, the authors explicitly identify Shaykh ʿUmar as leader (*amīr*). In fact, as late as sometime around 2003, Nājiḥ Ibrāhīm would state: "Were Shaykh ʿUmar among us, he would (formally) assume the leadership." See Aḥ mad, *Muʾāmarah,* 46.

66. See his *Kalimat al-ḥaqq: Murāfaʿāt al-duktūr ʿumar ʿabd al-raḥmān fī qaḍīyat al-jihād* (Cairo: Dār al-Iʿtisām, 1985).

67. According to the Stewart indictment, this was on September 20, 1999.

68. *Gamāʿah* leaders would later explain Shaykh ʿUmar's withdrawals as a function of the messenger, Aḥmad ʿAbd al-Sattār, intentionally passing bad intelligence to the shaykh. See Aḥmad, *Muʾāmarah,* 44–45.

69. According to the Stewart indictment, this was on June 20, 2000.

70. See *Nahr al-dhikrāyāt,* 35; al-ʿAwwā, *al-Jamāʿah,* 167. According to Zuhdī, however, the tour began in Ramaḍān (November–December) 2001. See Aḥmad, *Muʾāmarah,* 77. Meanwhile, Ashour, "Lions," 619, depicts the tour as taking place in 2002. Abū Zayd, *al-Jamāʿah al-islāmīyah,* 40, also gives January 2002 as the start date of the tour.

71. See note 4, above. Incidentally, Aḥmad was himself the victim of an assassination attempt, not by the *Gamāʿah* but by another radical Islamist group, *al-Nājūna min al-nār* (Those Spared Condemnation to Hell). See *Muʾāmarah,* 13.

72. In fact, see Zayyāt, *Road,* 80, where he states: "The imprisoned [al-]Gamāʿa al-Islāmīyya leaders are not easily coerced into anything that is against their beliefs. They have always had great courage in expressing their opinions and bearing the consequences both in times of war and in times of peace. . . . They have never bowed for a promise or a gift and they have learnt from the experiences of their predecessors that such promises are never kept." See also Aḥmad, *Muʾāmarah,* 167–68, for a similar assessment.

73. Cf., however, Ashour, "Lions," 621, 622, where it is claimed that the *Gamā'ah* leadership admits to succumbing to government repression. My difference with Ashour may be in the distinction between recognizing the fact and consequences of repression in general, and thus factoring this into the likely substance and duration of any reform effort, and seeing the *Gamā'ah* as actually succumbing to a campaign of repression that dictated a course of action that would otherwise not have been taken. After all, the fact that one is paranoid is not proof that one is not being followed.

74. In particular, he seems to resent the leadership's "dictatorial" style, its inflated claims regarding the profundity and uniqueness of its arguments and even the way they seemed to "work" the system in prison. For example, Munīb intimates that the leadership routinely adopted the practice of "sicking" the security apparatus on anyone who opposed or criticized the Initiative on charges of being *takfīrī*s (excommunicators) who deemed their opponents, including the government, to be apostate-infidels and thus lawful targets of attack. See Munīb, *Murāja'āt,* 35, 235, 240, 241, 242, and passim. According to E. Stein, Munīb was actually a "former Jihad member," though it was beyond the scope of his article to indicate when this affiliation began or ended. See E. Stein, "What Does the Gama'a Islamiyya Want Now?" *Middle East Report,* no. 254 (Spring 2010): 43.

75. Munīb, *Murāja'āt,* 8.

76. We might note in this context that while only *six* leaders attached their signatures to the original declaration read at court in 1997, the manifestos issued in 2002 carried the names of *eight* leaders.

77. Munīb, *Murāja'āt,* 8.

78. Ibid.

79. al-'Awwā, *al-Jamā'ah,* 161.

80. See ibid., 201. Ḥāfiẓ's comments are in Egyptian colloquial in the original Arabic text.

81. Ibid., 214 n. 285. In fact, in one of his letters, Rifāʿī Ṭāhā is explicit in his view that at the very least Ḥamdī ʿAbd al-Raḥmān and Usāmah Ḥafiẓ should refrain from signing any agreement to abandon violence because the fact that they were scheduled to be released from prison soon might make it appear to some, especially new and potential recruits, that they played ball. See Munīb, *Murājaʿāt,* 60. Of course, Ḥāfiẓ would ignore this and go on to endorse the Initiative. In fact, as noted earlier, the cover and title page of *Mubādarat waqf al-ʿunf* list him as one of its two coauthors, i.e., not just a signatory. See note 49 above.

82. See, e.g., al-ʿAwwā, *al-Jamāʿah,* 205–6.

83. See, e.g., ibid., 206.

84. Ibid., 200, relating the words of Maḥmūd Shuʿayb. See also Aḥ mad, *Muʾāmarah,* 122, for an independent corroboration of this same view.

85. Ibid., 204; emphasis mine.

86. Ibid., 205.

87. Ibid.

88. Ibid., 207; emphasis added. One notes, incidentally, that the fear that Yūsuf says he will set aside here is not of repression and the like but of criticism from and loss of reputation among Islamist peers and rivals.

89. This is the more conventional and specifically legalistic rendering of *maṣlaḥah,* to which I pay homage owing partly to the plainly legalistic thrust of the *Gamāʿah*'s effort.

90. The concept of *fiqh al-wāqiʿ* is actually not new. We find explicit expressions of it at least as far back as Ibn Qayyim al-Jawzīyah (d. 751/1350) in his reform-oriented work, *al-Ṭuruq al-Ḥukmīyah.* The term has come to enjoy in modern times, however, greater currency as a distinctly reform construct.

91. See the summary statement, at *Mubādarat,* 25.

92. Ibid., 39.

93. Ibid., 39–48.

94. *Taslīṭ*, 16–18.

95. This may have been a title applied to Ḥamdī among *Gamāʿah* members held along with him at *al-ʿAqrab* prison, but it seems to apply more generally to Nājiḥ Ibrāhīm, who seems to have emerged as the chief theoretician of the *Gamāʿah*.

96. Aḥmad, *Muʾāmarah*, 118. In other words, the assumption here is that the text will only say, "Fight the Jews," in order to realize some communal benefit or avert some communal harm. Thus, fighting them can only be carried out on the assumption that this benefit or harm will be realized or avoided, respectively. This, however, requires a proper assessment of the sociopolitical, economic and other circumstances on the ground.

97. *Taslīṭ*, 3. This, again, is the *primary* aim. The *Gamāʿah* would obviously not rule out the legitimacy of jihad as a means of repelling aggression, even where this was unrelated to propagating the Faith or "guiding humanity to God."

98. *Mubādarat*, 61, 62.

99. *Taslīṭ*, 3.

100. Ibid., 3–4.

101. *Mubādarat*, 58.

102. *Taslīṭ*, 49.

103. Alasdair MacIntyre characterizes Kant's "categorical imperative" as being impervious to any considerations beyond itself: "But the moral law must be entirely unvarying. When I have discerned a categorical imperative I have discerned a rule that has no exceptions. . . . Kant argues that my duty is my duty irrespective of the consequences, whether in this world or the next." See Alasdair MacIntyre, *A Short History of Ethics: A History of Moral Philosophy from the Homeric Age to the Twentieth Century*, 2nd ed. (Notre Dame, IN: University of Notre Dame Press, 2009), 195–96.

104. For an interesting comparison between the Egyptian and Islamic laws on adultery and fornication, see 'Umar 'Afīfī, *'A'shān mā tindirabsh 'alā afāk: Ḥaqquka ma'a al-shurṭah* (That You May Avoid Being Abused: Your Rights with the Police), 2nd ed. (Cairo: Maktabat Madbūlī, 2008), 190–202.

105. Incidentally, Munīb, *Murāja'āt,* 239, subtly misrepresents Ḥamdī on this point, claiming that the latter said that the ruler was "free to choose to apply *sharī'ah* or not, as he pleases."

106. Aḥmad, *Mu'āmarah,* 129–30. Ḥamdī continues: "It is the ruler's right to determine whether or not circumstances allow for the application of the rules of *sharī'ah.* And it is the duty of everyone to leave this determination to him (at least) regarding some matters, such as whether the country is vulnerable to outside attack or whether the presence of Christians in society or the presence of human rights organizations or the presence of the state of Israel next to us militate against the full application of *sharī'ah.* Still, as a Muslim, I cannot negate nor prorogue (the authority of) these rules, even as it is not my right to declare the ruler an Unbeliever simply because he sees broader aims and objectives that prevent him from applying them in certain areas." Aḥmad, *Mu'āmarah,* 130. We should note that the *Gamā'ah* also recognizes the validity of this logic in reverse, namely, that a ruler may wrongly institute rules that are on their face consistent with the religious law but whose social implications clearly imply a violation of the broader aims of the law itself. As a case in point, Usāmah Ḥafiẓ cites Kemal Atatürk's banning traditional turbans and imposing the wearing of Western-style hats. Clearly, Ḥāfiẓ notes, neither is the wearing of traditional turbans religiously required, nor is the wearing of a Western hat prima facie forbidden. In this particular concrete *context,* however, Atatürk's action was clearly an attempt to undermine indigenous cultural authority and open an Eastern Muslim society to the cultural hegemony and authority of the secularizing

West. Thus, it was proper at that time to condemn Atatürk's action of attempting to impose Western-style hats. Inasmuch, however, as the social circumstances have now changed to the point that wearing hats no longer have this connotation, it would be improper to hold to the *fatwā*s of those jurists who condemned this action as a violation of the religious law. See Aḥmad, *Mu'āmarah,* 36. Ultimately, without using the specific nomenclature, what the *Gamā'ah* is doing here is endorsing the classical doctrine of *siyāsah.* On *siyāsah,* see note 7 above.

107. In fact, in a newspaper interview in 2004, Karam Zuhdī noted that the international scene has now changed and that many Muslim governments face global pressures that prevent them from fully applying Islamic law. In this light, especially given the agenda of these "global hegemonic forces," it is incumbent upon Muslim activists to review their understanding of their relationship with Muslim governments. See *al-Multaqā al-dawlī*, March 17, 2004, p. 7.

108. 'Alī, *al-Haṣād al-murr,* 15.

109. Indeed, see the explicit statement on the power of nonviolence by Ṭāriq al-Zumar below. See also the view of Shaykh Yūsuf al-Qaraḍāwī on the diminishing role and relevance of jihad as armed conflict below, note 120.

110. *Istrātijīyah,* 8.

111. *Taslīṭ,* 7.

112. *Istrātijīyah,* 235, but see the entire discussion from 235–48. Elsewhere, Zuhdī equates modern visas with explicit grants of protection (*amān*) to non-Muslim tourists. This, he states, is a "modern rendering" of the traditional rules on grants of protection. See Aḥmad, *Mu'āmarah,* 95.

113. *Istrātijīyah,* 245. On this particular feature of the law of rebellion, see my "Domestic Terrorism in the Islamic Legal Tradition," *Muslim World* 91, nos. 3–4 (Fall 2001): 293–310.

114. One might note in this context Qur'ān 4:90: *Except those (Un-*

believers) who arrive at the camp of a group with whom you have a treaty or who come to you too contrite to fight either you or their own people. Had God willed, He would have given them the upper hand over you, in which case they would attack you. But if they move out of proximity to you, such that they would not attack you but would effectively declare peace with you, such people God has given you no right to attack.

115. *Istrātijīyah,* 247. Incidentally, at *Istrātijīyah,* 244, they point out that there are Muslims among "the Americans." Zuhdī himself reportedly has a sister who lives in the United States. See Aḥmad, *Mu'āmarah,* 49.

116. *Istrātijīyah,* 66–67. This was ratified in the so-called "Constitution of Medina." On the Constitution itself, see., e.g., R. B. Serjeant, "The Sunnah Jāmi'ah, Pacts with the Yathrib Jews, and the Tahrīm of Yathrib: Analysis and Translation of the Documents Comprised in the So-Called 'Constitution of Medina,'" *Bulletin of the School of Oriental and African Studies, University of London* 41, no. 1 (1978): 1–42.

117. For a cynical but pointed indictment of the hypocrisy with which the human rights regime is seen in Muslim lands and how it is rarely if ever applied to the plight of groups such as the *Gamā'ah,* despite the scope and nature of the sustained horrors they experience in Egyptian prisons, not to mention the extralegal detention and even execution of some of its members, see Ṭāriq al-Zumar, *Murāja'āt lā tarāju'āt* (Cairo: Dār Miṣr al-Maḥrūsah, 2008), 7–9.

118. See, e.g., *Nahr al-dhikrāyāt,* 231–34.

119. *Istrātijīyat,* 63.

120. One might note in this regard the recently stated view of Shaykh Yūsuf al-Qaraḍāwī, *Fiqh al-Jihād,* 2 vols. (Cairo: Maktabat Wahba, 2009), 1: 402–3, who suggests that instead of Muslims' singular preoccupation with military confrontation, the jihad of our times requires "a massive army of preachers, teachers, journalists and those who are competent in training people in how to address today's public

in the language of the age and the style of the times, through voice, image, spoken word, physical gesture, books, pamphlets, magazines, newspapers, dialogue, documentaries, drama, and motion pictures."

121. Aḥmad, *Mu'āmarah,* 133–34. Ḥamdī continues: "When Shaykh Usāmah b. Lādin wants to wage jihad, he does so with no consideration of the interests and harms that will accrue to his action. Thus, his action on September 11 struck down some six thousand [*sic*] Americans. But the result of this was the disappearance from the face of the earth of the (Islamic) nation of Afghanistan and the Ṭalibān government, to the point that Mulla 'Umar, the head of that government, had to flee on a motorcycle. And I believe that had Usāmah b. Lādin heard the voice of reason and the religious law (*ṣawt al-'aql wa al-shar'*), he would not have undertaken any of these actions, all of which have caused so much harm to the Muslims." Aḥmad, *Mu'āmarah,* 134. It should be noted that the *Gamā'ah*'s support for the Ṭalibān régime was merely as an Islamic state in general and did not extend to a blanket endorsement of all of the Ṭalibān's actions or policies. In fact, in an interview with 'Iṣām Darbālah (a first tier signatory of the series), in June 2002, the latter states explicitly that the *Gamā'ah* disagreed with any number of the Ṭalibān's "juristic choices." See *Istrātijīyah,* 347.

122. *Mubādarat,* 85.

123. Indeed, there are indications that the *Gamā'ah* leadership remained cognizant of certain problems attending its position on the status of Copts. According to Kamāl al-Sa'īd Ḥabīb, who, again, was a member of the original 1980 coalition, first-tier leader 'Āṣim 'Abd al-Mājid actually wrote a tract, *Īḍāḥ al-jawāb: Su'ālāt ahl al-kitāb* (Clarifying Responses: Questions Concerning the People of the Book), which was to be the fifth of the series of four manifestos issued in 2002. As of the time of Ḥabīb's writing in 2011, however, this tract had still not appeared, the *Gamā'ah* apparently recognizing that it con-

veyed sentiments to which Christians and secularists might strongly object. See Ḥabīb, "al-Ākhar," 156.

124. One might note in this context the hypothetical solution put forth by Shaykh Yūsuf al-Qaraḍāwī, i.e., that "protected minorities (*ahl al-dhimmah*) be exempted from the *jizya* in exchange for military service, it being viewed otherwise as the equivalent of obligatory alms (*zakāt*) extracted from Muslims." See Y. al-Qaraḍāwī, *al-Ḥurrīyah al-dīnīyah wa al-ta'addudīyah fī naẓar al-islām* (Beirut: al-Maktab al-Islāmī, 2007), 82.

125. *Mu'āmarah,* 56.

126. Ibid., 56–57. Makram continues: "And do you have enough money to do this?" Zuhdī responds, "We said, '*If* God enables us to do so.'" See also *Mu'āmarah,* 26–27, for a confirmation of this attitude on the part of the *Gamā'ah.* See also the teary-eyed apology, in 2002, of first-tier leader 'Iṣām Darbālah, in *Istrātijīyah,* 348.

127. Ashour, *Deradicalization,* 51–61; see also Zayyāt, *Road,* 79.

128. See, e.g., Aḥmad, *Mu'āmarah,* 49.

129. One should note, incidentally, that this did not go unanswered. Ayman al-Ẓawāhirī would pen a response to Dr. Faḍl entitled, *Al-Tabri'ah: Risālat tabri'at ummat al-qalam wa al-sayf min manqaṣat tuhmat al-khawar wa al-ḍa'f* (Exoneration: An Epistle Exonerating the Community of the Pen and Sword of the Blemishing Charge of Feebleness and Weakness).

130. Munīb, *Murāja'āt,* 275–76; *Dalīl,* 104–5.

131. See Ṭāriq al-Zumar, *Murāja'āt lā tarāju'āt,* 30. Though only twenty at the time, he was the bridge between 'Abd al-Salām Faraj and such high-profile figures as 'Abbūd al-Zumar (his cousin and a decorated military intelligence officer) and Khālid al-Islāmbūlī. While originally a member of *Tanẓīm al-Jihād,* he and his cousin defected in prison and joined the *Gamā'ah* in 1991. See Munīb, *Dalīl,* 179. Ṭāriq originally withheld support for the Initiative, but by the end of

1997 came to support it. Similarly, according to Munīb, *Dalīl,* 180–81, 'Abbūd, who was among the most influential jihadists in prison, merely supported the Initiative in order to strengthen the movement's bargaining power with the government. Ultimately, however, Ṭāriq would come to recognize the power of nonviolence, based on his own individual as well as his group's *experience.* Though he and his cousin had completed their sentences, Ṭāriq, e.g., by 2004 (Munīb, *Dalīl,* 184), both remained in prison as late as the end of 2010 with little hope of release. On March 14, 2011, however, following the nonviolent Egyptian revolution's first round of success, the *Gamā'ah*'s website streamed a hearty note of congratulations to Ṭāriq and 'Abbūd al-Zumar on their release from prison!

132. See, e.g., *Istrātijīyah,* 17: al-'Awwā, *al-Jamā'ah,* 152–59. See also Aḥmad, *Mu'āmarah,* 134–35, 168.

133. This may explain the palpable gap in America between those who are recognized by *Muslims* to represent Islam and those who are recognized by *non-Muslims* to represent Islam. There are simply informal bases of authority that are unconnected to Muslim tradition but are rooted in Western sensibilities (e.g., media savvy, "liberal" stands on hot-button issues) that are tapped into and deployed by the religiously untrained but largely ignored by the religiously trained. Thus, while the religiously trained outstrip their "lay" co-religionists in formal authority, the latter often outstrip the religiously trained, certainly where the audience is predominantly non-Muslim, in informal authority.

134. Etzioni, *Security First,* xiv–xvi.

Text

[The heading "Introduction" does not appear in the original. I add it here for consistency, the first heading in the original being "Chapter One."]

1. [For a brief glimpse into some of the theological implications of this notion, see my *Islam and the Problem of Black Suffering* (New York: Oxford University Press, 2009), 58–59, 82–83, and passim.]

2. *Ṣaḥīḥ al-Bukhārī* [5628]; *Ṣaḥīḥ Muslim* [190/146] on the authority of ʿAbd Allāh b. ʿAmr.

3. Narrated by al-Bukhārī [1509] and Muslim [1333/398].

4. ʿAbd al-Razzāq related on the authority of ʿAbd al-Malik b. Abī Bakr b. al-Ḥārith b. Hishām, who said, "ʿAyyāsh b. Abī Rabīʿah, Salamah b. Hishām and al-Walīd b. al-Walīd fled from the pagan idolaters. The Prophet• learned of their coming out (to the mosque) and supplicated when he raised his head from the bowing to the standing position in prayer." Ibn Isḥāq related from a hadith from Umm Salamah that she said to Salamah b. Hishām's wife, "Why do I not see Salamah praying with the Prophet•?" She responded, "Every time he comes out, the people yell, 'Runaway!'" That was after the campaign of Mu'tah. Al-Wāqidī related this from another channel, adding: "The Prophet• said, 'Nay, Oft-attacker.'" See *al-Iṣābah [fī tamyīz al-ṣaḥābah]*, 3:155. [I assume the reference here is to the work by this title by Ibn Ḥajar al-ʿAṣqalānī, though the authors give nothing beyond their reference to "*al-Iṣābah.*"]

5. Narrated by Aḥmad in *al-Musnad* [1/204]. Shaykh al-Arna'ūṭ added, "Its chain is sound, according to the standards of Muslim."

6. Al-ʿAjlūnī said in *Kashf al-khafā'* [2214]: "Aḥmad narrated this in The Book of Sunna on the authority of Ibn Masʿūd in the following words; 'Verily God surveyed the hearts of humanity and chose Muhammad•, thus dispatching him with His message. Then He surveyed the hearts of humanity again and chose companions for him, thus making them the supporters of His religion and the viziers of His prophet. Thus, what the Muslims deem to be good, it is good in the sight of God. And what they deem to be bad is bad in the sight of God." This report stops at a Companion, with a good (*ḥasan*)

chain. Al-Bazzār, al-Ṭayālisī, al-Ṭabarānī, Abū Na'īm and al-Bayhaqī, in his *al-I'tiqād (wa al-hidāyah ilā sabīl al-rashād)*, also narrate this on the authority of Ibn Mas'ūd. And in al-'Aynī's commentary on *al-Hidāyah,* we read that Aḥmad narrated through his chain on the authority of Ibn Mas'ūd: "God surveyed the hearts of humanity after having surveyed the heart of Muhammad•, and He found the hearts of the Companions to be the best hearts. So He made them the viziers of His prophet, who will fight in defense of His religion. Thus what the believers deem to be good is good in the sight of God. And what they deem to be evil—and in one narration, bad—is evil in the sight of God."

7. [*'Arāyah* (s. *'arīyah*) contracts entail a farmer donating stored, dried produce, and then buying it from the one to whom it was donated in exchange for dried produce from some future yield of his. While all *ribā* or unlawful increase may constitute a form of interest, not everything termed interest in a modern Western context, e.g., returns on stocks or the fixed marginal profit gained in a *murābahah* (profit-sharing) contract, necessarily constitutes a form of unlawful *ribā.*]

8. [*Gharar* refers to uncertainty in either of the counterexchanges in a sale or barter, i.e., either the price or the quality, quantity, or deliverability of the commodity. Thus, e.g., the ban on *gharar* would proscribe selling "thigamajigs" for one dollar or bread for "some money," or "a bird in the sky" for fifty dollars.]

9. In the commentary on *al-Mu'tamad fī uṣūl al-fiqh,* by Dr. Muḥ ammad al-Ḥabsh, we read: "Implicit interests are interests for the realization of which the Lawgiver has issued no explicit ruling, nor is there any direct scriptural proof indicating that they should be either recognized or ignored. Indeed, interests are of three types: (1) recognized interests, which the Lawgiver has explicitly identified, commanded, and called for their realization, such as with marriage,

travel, hunting, and the like; (2) unrecognized interests, which the Lawgiver explicitly proscribed and forbade, such as with *ribā* (interest?), gambling, and other such things; and (3) implicit interests, regarding which the Lawgiver remained silent, these interests constituting what are conventionally referred to as *maṣāliḥ mursalah*. Then he cited examples of implicit interests, such as systemizing the army, establishing military registries and setting up prisons for criminals—all of these interests being recognized by the Companions, though the Great Lawgiver remained silent about them. Then he noted that the legal theoreticians differ over the question of recognizing implicit interests as an independent proof in religious matters. Some count them as an independent proof; others count them as a corroborating proof that merely strengthens a conventionally recognized proof. And those who recognize the authority of implicit interests lay down three stipulations for doing so (1) that the interest be general, not specific (in scope); (2) that the interest be actual, not theoretical; and (3) that it not violate a recognized legal principle. And according to the advocates of these interests, there are four considerations that compel one to invoke them: (1) averting harm from the people; (2) blocking legal means to ends that result in harm and sin; (3) procuring the interests of the people; and (4) changes in time that result in the emergence of new interests for the people. [The logic here, incidentally, is similar to that indulged by the U.S. Supreme Court in recognizing "unenumerated rights," e.g., the right to privacy, that are derived on the basis of the principle of "substantive due process."]

10. See *al-Muʿtamad fī uṣūl al-fiqh*, question 140 in the introduction to the broader aims and objections of the law (*maqāṣid al-sharīʿah*).

11. Ibid., question 141.

12. Al-Bukhārī narrated [4701] that Zayd b. Thābit,° said: "Abū Bakr sent for me on the occasion of the death of those who fell at al-Yamāmah, and I found ʿUmar b. al-Khaṭṭāb in his presence. Abū

Bakr° said, ' 'Umar has come to me saying, "Death at al-Yamāmah has decimated the Qur'ān readers. And I fear that death might decimate the Qur'ān readers at other places as well, as a result of which much of the Qur'ān ends up lost. Thus, it is my view that you should order that the Qur'ān be collected [in written form]."' I (Zayd) said to 'Umar, 'How can you do something that the Prophet• did not do?' 'Umar responded, 'By God, this is a good thing,' and he continued to prompt me until God opened my breast to the idea and I came to see what 'Umar saw in it." Zayd said, "Abū Bakr said to me, 'You are an intelligent young man of whose integrity we have no doubt. You used to write down the revelations for the Prophet•. So, go track down the Qur'ān and gather it (into a compendium).' And by God, had they charged me with moving a mountain, that would not have weighed heavier on me than his ordering me to collect the Qur'ān. I said, 'How can you do something that the Prophet did not do?' He responded, 'By God, this is a good thing.' And Abū Bakr continued to prompt me until God opened my breast to the idea to which He had opened the breast of Abū Bakr and 'Umar°. So I tracked down the Qur'ān, gathering it from stripped palm branches, stones, and the breasts of men, until I found the last part of *Sūrat al-Tawbah,* which I found with no one else, with Abū Khuzaymah al-Anṣārī: {*Indeed, a prophet from among yourselves has come to you, who is anguished by the difficulties you encounter*} [9:128] up to the end of *Barā'ah.* These 'pages' remained with Abū Bakr until his death. Then they passed to 'Umar for the duration of his life. Then they passed to Ḥafṣah, the daughter of 'Umar°."

13. [This is actually the position of al-Ghazālī, who was a Shāfi'ī in law and more positivist in approach. Other schools, especially Mālikīs and Ḥanbalīs, have a more indulgent attitude towards setting aside or promulgating rules based on *maṣlaḥah mursalah.* The Ḥanafī's, meanwhile, are often equally indulgent on the basis of the principle

of *istiḥsān* or "equity." See, e.g., Wahbah al-Zuḥaylī, *Uṣūl al-fiqh al-islāmī*, 2 vols. (Damascus: Dār al-Fikr, 1431/2010), 2: 34–63.]

14. See *Majmū' fatāwā shaykh al-islām aḥmad ibn taymīya*, 37 vols. (N.p.: N.d), 5: 48.

15. [This entire section is placed between quotations in the original, though no reference is given in the notes. One assumes the quote is a continuation from Ibn Taymīya.]

16. [For a useful clarification on the application of this principle, see number 107 below. We might note, meanwhile, a difference between applying this principle to groups versus individuals. Where an individual Muslim is pressured to abandon his religion on pain of death, the religious law places life above religion and sanctions the outward renunciation of Islam. See, e.g., Qur'ān 16:106.]

17. [See appendix.]

18. [*Al-ḍarb fī suwādā' al-qalb* was a phrase reportedly coined by minister of the interior Zakī Badr to refer to the practice of abusing, humiliating, and torturing family members, including women and children, in order to get suspected members of the *Gamā'ah* to confess. See Abū Zayd, "al-Jamā'ah al-islāmīyah," 33.]

19. Muslim related [2888/14] on the authority of Abū Bakrah° that he said: "The Prophet• said, 'There will be strife. Do I not say that there will be strife in which those who sit during it are better than those who walk in it, and those who walk in it are better than those who run to it. Do I not say that if this strife comes upon you or happens in your presence, then whoever has camels, let him return to his flock, and whoever has goats, let him return to his flock, and whoever has land, let him return to his land.'" Abū Bakrah continued, "A man then said, 'O Messenger of God, what of he who has no camels, no goats or no land?' The Prophet replied, 'Let him repair to his sword and pound its blade with rocks. Then, if he is able, let him escape. My Lord, have I not made it clear? My Lord, have I not made it clear?

My Lord, have I not made it clear?' So a man said, 'O Messenger of God, what if I am coerced to the point that I am taken to one side, or one party, and a man strikes me with his sword or an arrow comes and kills me?' The Prophet replied, 'He shall incur his sin as well as your sin, and he shall be among the companions of Hell.'"

20. [Simon and Schuster, 1992.]

21. [This was the attempt by minister of interior 'Abd al-Ḥalīm Mūsā. See al-'Awwā, *al-Jamā'ah,* 152.]

22. A proverb cited by al-Mundhirī, who said, "This is among their well-known proverbs as appears in al-Maydānī's *al-Amthāl.*"

23. Linguistically speaking, a "cause" is that through which one arrives at one's intended goal. In the terminology of the legal theoreticians, however, it refers to a manifest, palpable phenomenon, which the Lawgiver has rendered an indication of the applicability of a particular rule, its existence entailing its applicability, its absence entailing the absence thereof. In his definition, Dr. 'Abd al-Wahhāb Khallāf stated, "It is every thing the Lawgiver has rendered an indication of a particular effect, tying its existence to the existence of this effect and its absence to its absence." This is like the Lawgiver rendering the sun passing its zenith a legal cause obligating the performance of the noon prayer or a sign indicating this obligation, its existence entailing the existence of this obligation and its absence entailing its absence. Similarly, the Lawgiver has rendered aggressive, intentional homicide a legal cause obligating the offering of retaliatory options (*qiṣāṣ*).

24. Narrated by al-Bukhārī [123] on the authority of Abū Mūsā°.

25. Narrated by al-Bukhārī [2600] and Muslim [1904] on the authority of Abū Mūsā°.

26. This is part of a hadith related by al-Bukhārī [3489] and Muslim [34/240] on the authority of Sahl b. Sa'd°.

27. This is part of a hadith related by Muslim [16/2674] on the authority of Abū Hurayrah.

28. This is a reference to The Exalted's statement, *And if anyone from among the pagan associationists should seek asylum with you, grant it to him that he may hear the Word of God. Then, deliver him to safe quarters. That is because they are a people who know not* [9: 6]. Al-Qurṭ ubī said: "If among those whom I have commanded you to fight one {"seeks asylum with you"}, i.e., he asks for asylum, which is protection and security of life, grant it to him so that he can hear the Qur'ān, i.e., that he can understand its judgments, commands, and prohibitions. If he accepts any of this, fine. If he rejects it, return him to safe quarters. This is an issue on which there is no difference of opinion." He also said: "And there is no difference of opinion among all of the scholars that it is permissible for the ruler to grant such protection. For he is the one put forth to investigate matters and determine communal interests. And he represents the Community in procuring interests and averting harms."

29. Imām al-Qurṭubī stated: "There is no disagreement that fighting was prohibited before the migration to Medina, in accordance with His statement, *Repel (their aggression) with what is more seemly* [23:96], and His statement, *Pardon them and forgive* [5:13], and His statement, *Take leave of them with indulgence* [73:10], and His statement, *You are not a master over them* [88:22], and other such verses revealed at Mecca."

30. The hadith expert Ibn Ḥajar (d. 852/1448) stated in his book *Fatḥ al-bārī,* in the chapter on military campaigns, under the segment heading, "The Killing of Ḥamza b. 'Abd al-Muṭṭalib°": "On the authority of Yūnus b. Bakīr from the book *al-Maghāzī* (on military campaigns), by Ibn Isḥāq, who said; 'It was said to the Messenger of God•, "There is Waḥshī (the man who killed the Prophet's uncle, Ḥamza)!" The Prophet responded, "Leave him; for, indeed, it is more beloved to me for a single man to embrace Islam than killing a thousand Unbelievers."'"

31. [Al-Shawkānī's point here is not that context is irrelevant to determining general meaning but that what "self-destruction" or "property" may have meant at the time of revelation does not limit what we can apply the terms "self-destruction" or "property" (or the rules governing these) to today.]

32. Al-Bukhārī [3936] and Muslim [1860/80] narrated on the authority of Yazīd b. Abī 'Ubayd: "I said to Salamah b. al-Akwa', 'What did you pledge to the Prophet• on the day of al-Ḥudaybīyah?' He said, 'To defend him to the death.'"

33. [A reference to a famous treaty contracted between the Prophet and Quraysh in the sixth year after the Migration to Medina.]

34. [The quoted segment is from Abū 'Abd Allāh Muḥammad b. Aḥmad al-Anṣārī al-Qurṭubī's *al-Jāmi' li aḥkām al-qur'ān*, 11 vols. (Beirut: Dār al-Fikr, 1420/1999), 8:206. I have not been able to identify this Abū Zayd, but it is certainly not the famed Ibn Abī Zayd al-Qayrawānī, as the latter died in 386/996, whereas Ibn al-Qāsim died in 191/806.]

35. This is part of a hadith related by al-Bukhārī [1335] and Muslim [20/32]. [Meanwhile, Shaykh Yūsuf al-Qaraḍāwī recently discussed this report in a manner that might provide useful clarification. He notes that there has never been a consensus among the doctors of the law that "the people" (*al-nās*) here means "mankind" or "all the people of the world." In fact, he insists, "no scholar of this Community has ever held this view, not a jurist, not an exegete, not a hadith expert." He reminds his reader that the definite article in Arabic (such as placed before "the people" in this hadith) can be used to denote a general or a specific category and that the general consensus is that it is used here to refer specifically to the pagan Arabians who refused peaceful coexistence with the Prophet. Beyond this, he cites, inter alia, the view of Ibn Taymīya to the effect that the hadith merely binds the Prophet to a specific *goal* in fighting those he fights, that is, as a

means of facilitating their way to Islam, as opposed to merely despoiling them of their wealth or lording over them politically. Indeed, Ibn Taymīya insists, "This [war-against-the-entire-world rendering of the hadith] would violate scripture and unanimous consensus. For he [the Prophet] never did this. Rather, his way was to refrain from fighting those who conducted themselves peacefully towards him." See Yūsuf al-Qaraḍāwī, *Fiqh al-jihād,* 2 vols. (Cairo: Maktabat Wahba, 1430/2009), 1: 327–37, esp. 1: 327 and 1: 335, for the quoted segments, respectively.]

36. Narrated by al-Bukhārī [3794] and Muslim [95/155].

37. Muslim [96/158] and al-Bukhārī [4021] narrate this.

38. Al-Bukhārī [384] narrated this.

39. Muslim [3/1731] narrated this.

40. This is part of a hadith narrated by al-Bukhārī [2989].

41. See note 39, above, on the provenance of this hadith.

42. This hadith is commonly traced to Mālik's *al-Muwaṭṭa'*. There, however, a slightly different wording appears without any mention of execution: "'Should you not have sequestered him in a house for three days, fed him a loaf of bread each day while asking him to repent, perhaps he might repent and restore himself to the command of God?' 'Umar then said, 'My Lord, I was not present, nor did I command this, nor did it please me when it reached my attention.'" See *al-Muwaṭṭa'*, ed. M. F. 'Abd al-Bāqī (Cairo: Dār Iḥyā' al-Kutub al-'Arabīyah, N.d), 2:737. Meanwhile, in his commentary on this section of Shirāzī's *al-Muhadhdhab,* al-Nawawī (a Shāfi'ī) traces the hadith to narrations from al-Shāfi'ī (on the authority of Muḥammad b. 'Abd Allāh b. 'Abd al-Qārī) and Mālik (on the authority of 'Abd al-Raḥ mān b. Muḥammad b. 'Abd Allāh b. 'Abd al-Qārī from the latter's father). Again, however, this narration makes no mention of execution. See Abū Zakarīyā Muḥyī al-Dīn b. Sharaf al-Nawawī, *Kitāb al-majmū' sharḥ al-muhadhdhab li al-shirāzī*, 23 vols., ed. M. N. al-Muṭī'ī

(Cairo: Dār Iḥyā' al-Turāth al-'Arabī, 1415/1995), 21:62–64, esp. 63–64. For a modern juristic challenge to the classical rule holding apostasy to be a capital offense, see Ṭ. J. al-'Alwānī, *Lā ikrāha fī dīn: ishkālīyat al-riddah wa al-murtaddīn min ṣadr al-islām ilā al-yawm,* 2nd ed. (Cairo: Maktabat al-Shurūq al-Dawlīyah, 1427/2006).

43. [A campaign conducted in year 7 A.H. against the Jewish tribe of Banū Naḍīr, who had initiated the infamous "Siege of Medina," involving the Jews, the Banū Ghaṭafān, and Quraysh against the Prophet in Medina.]

44. Part of a hadith related by al-Bukhārī [3010–11] and Muslim [1785/94] on the authority of Sahl b. Ḥunayf°.

45. See note 5, above, on the provenance of this hadith.

Appendix

1. This is a standard prioritization according to the Ḥanafī school. Mālikīs and Ḥanbalīs, meanwhile, are known to place sanity over progeny. See, e.g., al-Zuḥaylī, *Uṣūl al-fiqh,* 2: 33 n. 3.

Index

Names beginning with "Ibn" in index may appear with abbreviated "b." before the name in the text.

al-Ghazālī (Abū Ḥāmid), 62, 150*n*13
al-Ghazālī, Muḥammad, 46
Government role
ceding authority to, 34
establishment of state, 61
exploiting of the Initiative, 43
fighting between Muslims and police officers and officials, 9, 11, 84, 130*n*34
Islamic rules on crimes and, 33–34
motivations for the Initiative not due to coercion or manipulation by, 21–24, 126*n*7, 137*n*72, 139n81
response to September 11, 2001, terrorist attacks, 19
Guiding humanity as mission, 87–90, 113

Ḥabīb, Kamāl al-Sa'īd, 5, 127*n*13, 144*n*123
al-Ḥabsh, Muḥammad, 148*n*9
Ḥāfiẓ, Usāmah Ibrāhīm, 10, 11, 24, 132*n*42, 133*n*49, 134*n*53, 139*n*81, 141*n*106
Hamza, Muṣṭafā, 135*n*58
Ḥanafī school, 156*n*1
Ḥanbalīs, 150*n*13, 156*n*1
Harm. *See* Avoidance of harm
al-Ḥaṣkafī, Muḥammad b. 'Alā' al-Dīn, 91
al-Ḥaṣkafī, Shaykh, 104, 110
Hirelings, liability of, 60
Hishām, Maslamah b., 97
Hishām, Salamah b., 147*n*4
Historical evolution, 3–12
Historical Leadership of the *Gamā'ah,* 13, 15–17, 19–22, 52
coercion and weakness not factor in agreeing to the Initiative, 21–24, 137*n*72, 139*n*81
main argument for the Initiative, 27–40
and religious basis for the Initiative, 23, 46
Rifā'ī Ṭāhā's role in, 135*nn*58–59
texts used by, 48
al-Ḥukāymah, Muḥammad Khalīl, 136*n*60
Human rights regime, 39, 141*n*106, 143*n*117
Human shields, 98
Huwaydī, Fahmī, 46

Ibn 'Abd al-Salām, 'Izz al-Dīn, 92
Ibn Abī Ḥātim, 94
Ibn 'Ābidīn, 85, 91, 104, 108, 110
Ibn 'Adī, 'Ubayd Allāh, 99
Ibn al-Akwa', Salamah , 154*n*32
Ibn al-'Arabī, Abū Bakr, 98
Ibn al-'Āṣ, 'Amr, b., 94
Ibn al-Aswad, Miqdād b., 100
Ibn al-Aswad b. 'Abd Yaghūth, 'Abd al-Raḥmān, 94
Ibn Ḥabīb, 111
Ibn Ḥajar (al-'Aṣqalānī), 153*n*30
Ibn Ḥanbal, Aḥmad b. (al-Imām), 111
Ibn Isḥāq, Muḥammad, 89, 147*n*4

Prisons/prisoners
acknowledging mistake of violent confrontation, 43
al-'Aqrab prison, 25–26, 140*n*95
Gamā'ah members, 7, 11–12, 145*n*131
jailhouse "rep," importance to prisoners, 23–24
length of sentence/detention, 131*n*37
Līmān Ṭurah prison, 24, 25
plight of incarcerated, 54, 66–67
release after Egyptian revolution (2011), 145*n*131
release after Luxor massacre (1997), 134*n*56
tour of Historic Leadership to, 19, 20, 137*n*70
al-Wādī al-Jadīd prison, 24
Privacy in U.S. as constitutional right, 149*n*9
Private interests distinguished from implicit interests, 63
Propaganda
Israel spreading, 72–73
removal of minister of the interior due to, 78
Prophet
chosen as Messenger, 147*n*6
courage of, 113
extending invitation to Islam prior to fighting, 89, 107
on humiliation, 115
on *jizya* (religious tax paid by non-Muslims), 103
on nonviolence toward peaceable peoples, 155*n*35
on passivity in the face of strife, 150*n*19
treaties and pacts with non-Muslims, 38, 113
on unbeliever stating acceptance of true faith, 100, 153*n*30
valuing fundamental interests over cosmetic interests, 118–119
Prophets' purpose to deliver message of call to God, 89, 113
Protection of non-Muslims. See *Jizya*

al-Qā'idah
comparison of the Initiative's visions with, 35–36
defeat of America and the West as goal of, 39–40
defecting *Gāmā'ah* members joining, 136*n*60
misunderstanding of jihad, 36–37, 39
overinclusive jihad targets innocent civilians, 36–37
Tanẓīm al-Jihād members joining, 129*n*27
Western view of, 1–2
Al-Qā'idah's Strategy and Bombings: Mistakes and Dangers [*Istrātījīyah wa tafjīrāt al-Qā'idah: al-Akhṭā' wa al-akhṭār*], 36
al-Qamarī, 'Iṣām, 5
al-Qaraḍāwī, Yūsuf, 115, 143*n*120, 145*n*124, 154*n*35
Qur'ān
collection after death of the Prophet, 63, 150*n*12
interpretation to suit views, 48